Emma Seiler, William H. Furness

The Voice in Speaking

Emma Seiler, William H. Furness

The Voice in Speaking

ISBN/EAN: 9783743329959

Manufactured in Europe, USA, Canada, Australia, Japa

Cover: Foto ©ninafisch / pixelio.de

Manufactured and distributed by brebook publishing software (www.brebook.com)

Emma Seiler, William H. Furness

The Voice in Speaking

THE

VOICE IN SPEAKING

TRANSLATED FROM THE GERMAN OF

EMMA SEILER

MEMBER OF THE AMERICAN PHILOSOPHICAL SOCIETY AND AUTHOR OF
"THE VOICE IN SINGING"

BY

W. H. FURNESS D.D.

MEMBER OF THE AMERICAN PHILOSOPHICAL SOCIETY

PHILADELPHIA
J. B. LIPPINCOTT & CO.
1875

Entered, according to Act of Congress, in the year 1874, by
J. B. LIPPINCOTT & CO.,
In the Office of the Librarian of Congress at Washington.

CONTENTS.

	PAGE
INTRODUCTION	5

CHAPTER I.
ACOUSTICS IN GENERAL 11

CHAPTER II.
THE VOWELS 23

CHAPTER III.
THE CONSONANTS 34

CHAPTER IV.
THE VOCAL TONES 62

CHAPTER V.
THE TIMBRE OF THE VOICE 85

CHAPTER VI.
REACH OF THE VOICE 95

CHAPTER VII.
THE REFLECTION OF SOUND 102

CHAPTER VIII.

FAULTS IN SPEAKING 131

CHAPTER IX.

MODULATION 131

APPENDIX.

CLERGYMAN'S SORE THROAT, BY CARL SEILER, M.D. 155

INTRODUCTION.

SINCE the publication of "The Voice in Singing," I have frequently been applied to for information and instruction by teachers of elocution and by persons whose callings require them to speak in public. My attention has thus been turned to the action of the Voice in Speaking; and occasion has been afforded me to pursue more thoroughly, with the assistance of my son, Dr. Carl Seiler, the study of the natural laws underlying these sounds. The results which we have arrived at are given in the first part of this little work.

As at the present day, with advancing intellectual culture, it becomes more and more the aim of individuals to give a higher and more graceful character to the various modes of expressing the inner life, so was it likewise, as history bears witness, among the most cultivated nations of ancient times. In every civilized people the endeavor to perfect the manner of speaking is always especially conspicuous. Of all our ways of giving utterance to the life within, Speech is the most important. It is the minister of our collective intellectual being. This it is that raises man above all other living creatures and renders him capable of constant and illimitable progress, making the conquests of one the property of all.

So long ago as the fifth century before Christ there were schools in Greece in which the Art of Speaking was taught. In the convent schools of the Middle Ages it was carefully cultivated, just as at the present day it is made a branch of study in most of the educational institutions of Europe.

But, although the Art of Speaking has been so long taught, there has been no guiding principle in the work of instruction. The sole reliance has been a more or less obscure sense of the beautiful. The examples of distinguished orators and dramatic artists have alone been looked to. The method of teaching has been purely empirical; and the true and the beautiful in speaking have been unconsciously reached by renowned speakers and actors only by the sure instinct of genius.

INTRODUCTION. 7

In works upon Elocution attention is almost exclusively given to the so-called Modulation of the Voice, to Expression and whatever pertains thereto; while sonorousness and fulness of voice are regarded as incidental gifts of Nature, admitting neither of modification nor of improvement. As to distinctness and reach of voice,—these, it is considered, are attainable only by the exertion of mere physical force.

It is only recently that Science has succeeded in discovering and elucidating the natural laws upon which all the sounds of the human voice depend. *These laws of Nature are, in both sexes and in all mankind of every* **age and tongue,** *unchangeably the same,* irrespective of the manner in which these sounds may be combined in different languages. Every normal human being is by nature capable of forming all the sounds that occur in the various tongues and dialects of mankind, although all the sounds capable of being made by the voice do not appear in any one language.

With an accurate knowledge of the laws upon which melody, fulness, distinctness, reach of voice, etc., depend, it becomes possible to communicate these qualities to voices to which they do not appear naturally to belong.

Prof. Helmholtz, in his work "*Die Lehre von den Tonempfindungen,*" in which are published his investigations of the vowel sounds, was the first to call attention to the musical properties of the speaking sounds of the human voice. But although, since the appearance of that great work, Acoustics, physically and physiologically considered, have been made the subject of new and diligent study, and much valuable information has been obtained in this department of natural science, yet, with a single exception,* no attempt has thus far been made, with favorable results, to ascertain, for the perfecting of the power of speech, the musical character of consonant sounds.†

It was with this in view that, with the aid of my son, I began the preparation of this book, the labor of which was at first not a little increased

---

* Dr. Oscar Wolf: *Sprache und Ohr.*

† Jacob Grimm, the most eminent of German students of language, disposes of the influence of physical Acoustics in the improvement of the speaking voice with the jesting remark that "the air was too thin a thing for him."

by the many obscurities and contradictions that tended to lead us astray. In investigating the musical qualities of the sounds of Speech, we made use of a series of tuning-forks and resonators, and had advanced a considerable way in our inquiries when there appeared the valuable work by Dr. Wolf, of Frankfort, just referred to, in which this portion of our general subject is treated with like results: one of many instances, by the way, of the occurrence of the same thought coincidently to different persons in different places and of the adoption of similar methods of developing it.

Although Dr. Wolf has studied the musical qualities of the Consonants only with reference to morbid conditions of the sense of hearing, he has nevertheless pursued his inquiries in the same way as ourselves, and, with slight variations, has arrived at the same conclusions.

Dr. Wolf has had the advantage of the Overtone Apparatus, recently invented by Appun in Hanau, by which the labor of the inquiry was materially lightened. The fact, however, that, pursuing this study independently of each other and with different aids, we have come to so close an agreement in our results, is no slight testimony to their correctness.

As Dr. Wolf was the first to publish his work, to him is due the credit of being *the first to discover and describe the musical character of the Consonants.*

This is, however, only a part of the task undertaken in this book, which is to investigate specially those functions of our vocal organs not hitherto understood, and to elucidate the results of these investigations as clearly as possible, and so to open a road for the improvement of our mode of speaking.

THE VOICE IN SPEAKING.

CHAPTER I.

ACOUSTICS IN GENERAL.

IN order to be able to give a clear idea of the interesting processes of the organs of the human voice in the act of speaking, we must go back, at the risk of repeating what is well known, to Acoustics in general, as elucidated by Prof. Helmholtz.

The movements of the air, which convey sound to our ears, come to us in two forms, as Tone and as Noise.* The whistling of the wind, the splashing of water, the rattling of a wagon, are noises. Musical instruments give us tones. When, however, many untuned instruments sound together, or when all the keys of a piano within an octave are struck at the same time, then it is

* The Voice in Singing, by E. Seiler.

a noise that we hear. Tones are therefore more simple and regular than noises. The ear perceives both by means of the agitation of the air that surrounds us. In the case of noise, the agitation of the air is an irregularly changing motion. In musical sounds, on the other hand, there is a movement of the air in a continuously regular manner, which must be caused by a similar movement in the body which gives the sound. These so-called periodical movements of the sounding body, rising, falling, and repeated at equal intervals, are named vibrations. The length of the interval elapsing between one movement and the next succeeding repetition of the same movement is called the duration of vibration, or period of motion.

A Tone is produced by a periodical motion of the sounding body; a Noise, by motions not periodical. We can see and feel the sounding vibrations of stationary bodies. The eye can perceive the vibrations of a string, and a person playing on a clarionet, an oboe, or any similar instrument, feels the vibration of the reed in the mouth-piece. How the movements of the air, agitated by the vibrations of the stationary body, are felt by the ear as Tone, Helmholtz illustrates by the motion of waves of water, in the following way. Imagine a stone thrown into perfectly smooth water. Around the point of the surface struck by the stone there is instantly formed a little ring, which, moving outward equally in all directions, spreads to an ever-enlarging circle. Corresponding with this ring, sound-waves go out in the air from an agitated point, and enlarge in all directions as far as the limits of the atmosphere permit. What goes on in the air is essentially the same that takes place on the surface of the water; the chief difference only is, that sound spreads out in the spacious sea of air like a sphere, while the waves on the surface of the water can extend only like a circle. At the surface, the mass of the water is free to rise upward, where it is compressed and forms billows or crests. In the interior of the aerial ocean the air must be condensed, because it cannot rise; for, in fact, the condensation of the sound-wave corresponds with the crest, while the rarefaction of the sound-wave corresponds with the sinus of the water-wave.* The water-waves press continually onwards into the distance, but the particles of the water move up and down periodically within

* Tyndall.

narrow limits. **One** may easily see these two movements by observing a small piece of wood floating on water: **the wood** moves just as the **particles of** water in contact with it move. It is not carried along with the rings of the wave, but is tossed up and down, and at last remains in the same place where it was at first. In a similar way, as the particles of water around **the wood are moved by** the ring only in passing, **so the** waves of sound spread onwards through new strata of air, while the particles of air, tossed to and fro by these waves as they pass, are never really moved by them from their first place. **A** drop falling upon the surface of the water creates in it only a single agitation; but when **a regular series of drops falls** upon it, every drop **produces a** ring on the water, every ring passes over **the surface** just like its predecessor, and is followed **by other rings in the** same way. In this way there is produced **on** the water a regular series of rings **ever expanding.** As many drops as fall into the **water in** a second, so many waves will in a second strike a floating piece of wood, which will be just so **many times tossed** up and down, and thus have a **periodical motion, the period of which** corresponds

ACOUSTICS IN GENERAL. 15

with the interval at which the drops fall. In like manner a sounding body periodically moved produces a similar periodic movement: **first of the air,** and then of the drum in the **ear;** the duration of the vibrations constituting the movement must be the same in the ear as in the sounding body.

The sounds produced by such periodic **agitations** of the air have three properties: **1. Strength;** 2. Pitch; 3. **Timbre.**

The Strength of the tone depends on the greater or less breadth of its vibrations,—that is, of the waves of **sound;** the higher or lower pitch of the tones, upon the number of vibrations,—that is, the tones **are always higher** the greater the number, and lower the fewer.

A second is used as the unit of time, **and by number of** vibrations is understood **the number** which the sounding body gives forth **in a** second **of time.** The tones used in music lie between 40 and 4000 vibrations per second in the extent of seven octaves. The tones which we can perceive lie between 16 and 38,000 vibrations to the second within the compass of eleven octaves. The one-lined a from **which all** instruments are tuned, has now usually 440 to 450 vibrations to the second in England and America. The French Academy, however, has recently established for the same note 435 vibrations, and this lower tuning has already been universally introduced in Germany.*

The octave of a tone has in the same time exactly twice as many vibrations as the tone itself. The fifth above the first octave has three times as many; the second octave, four times; the major third above the second octave, five times; the fifth of the same octave, six times; and the minor seventh of the same octave, seven times. In notation it would be thus, taking as the lowest note C, for example:

* Radau, in his "*L'Acoustique ou les Phénomènes du Son,*" states the difference between the concert pitch and the natural pitch to be, as is shown in the following scale, within an octave:

ACOUSTICS IN GENERAL. 17

The figures below the lines denote how many times **greater the number of** vibrations is than that of the first tone. In the **first** octave we find only one tone; in the second, two; in **the** third, all **the tones** of **the** major chord with the minor seventh. In the fourth octave **we** find eight tones, which, however, **we** divide **in our** system of music **into** twelve. **Likewise, there are in** the **fifth octave sixteen** tones, which number **is** doubled in the sixth. **Hence** the Greeks, following **the** natural laws **of** Acoustics, had quarter and eighth tones, which **we**, in our moderated scale, have done away with.*

The production of a higher **pitch in a** tone depends in all sounding bodies upon the uniform **law** which **we** may observe in the strings **of musical** instruments, whose tones ascend either **by** greater tension, by shortening, or through a diminution of the density **of the** strings. **It** is the **same** with sounding air-columns, as in organ-pipes and flutes,

---

* **So long as** melody alone was aimed at in music, and was accompanied only by octaves, the tones preserved their natural purity. But with the rise of harmony (the accord of different tones) there was rendered necessary a more regular system, to which the purity of the tones was sacrificed.

the vocal cords of the human voice, and all tone-producing bodies.

Strength and Pitch are the first two properties of Sound. The third property of Sound is the **Timbre. When we hear one and the same tone sounded successively** upon a violin, trumpet, clarionet, oboe, piano, by a human **voice, etc.,** although the tone is of the same strength and pitch, **yet the** character of it is different, and we very easily **distinguish** the instrument from which it comes. The **changes of the timbre** seem to be infinitely manifold, for, **not to mention the fact that** we have a **multitude** of different musical instruments all of **which can** give the same tone, and that different instruments of the same kind as well as different voices show certain differences of Timbre, the very **same** tone **can** be **given upon** one and the same instrument, **or by** one and **the** same voice, with many differences of Timbre. Since now the strength of the tone is determined by the breadth (amplitude) **of** the vibrations, **and** the pitch by their number, so the varieties of Timbre are owing to the different **forms of** the sound-waves; for, as the surface of the water is stirred differently by the falling into it of a stone, by the blowing over it of the wind, and by the passing through it of a ship, etc., so the movements of the air take different shapes from sounding bodies. The movement proceeding from the string of a violin over which the bow is drawn is different from that caused by the hammer of a piano or by a clarionet.

That Timbre is dependent on the form of the vibrations is confirmed by Helmholtz, and acknowledged as so far correct that every different timbre requires a different vibratory form; but different forms sometimes correspond to nearly the same timbre. We have learned by the stereoscope that we perceive two different views of every object, and that we compose a third one from those two. In like manner the ear perceives different tones which come to our consciousness only as one tone.

It is in general very difficult, especially in the case of the human voice, to distinguish these single parts of tone, because we are accustomed to take the impressions of the external world without analyzing them, and only for the sake of their practical utility.

But when we are once convinced of the existence of partial tones, we can, if we concentrate our attention, also distinguish them.* The ear hears, then, not only that tone the pitch of which is determined, as we have shown, by the number of its vibrations, but a whole series of tones besides, which are named "*the Harmonics, or overtones*," of the tone, which are arranged in a certain order above the first or fundamental tone, which is generally the strongest.

Helmholtz has shown that all sounds have overtones, which are a production of sound forming itself in the air. But to dwell upon this point here would lead us too far away. The series of these overtones has for each perfect musical tone the same order which has already been given (p. 16). Imperfect musical tones contain so-called inharmonic overtones, which lie close together higher than the harmonic overtones, and hence cause the lower harmonic overtones to be weak or to disappear altogether. The different timbre of tones thus depends upon the different forms of the

---

* When we strike strongly on the piano the low contra C and press the pedal at the same time, and then silence the string of the struck note with the finger, we hear quite plainly several overtones as soon as the fundamental tone ceases to overpower them.

ACOUSTICS IN GENERAL. 21

vibrations, **whence arise various relations** of the fundamental **tone to** the overtones, as they vary **in** strength and number. The most thorough inquiries have led to the following results, **of the first** importance in every formation **of** tone: *that the appropriate form of the vibratory* **waves, which** *is the most agreeable to the* **ear, as** *well* **as the** *fullest, softest, and* **most** *beautiful* **timbre which corresponds to that** *form,* **is** *produced when the fundamental* **tone and** *its overtones so sound* **that** *the fundamental* **tone** *and the overtones are perceived together, the former most strongly, while the latter are heard more and more faintly in the* **intervals** *of the major chord with the minor seventh, so that with the fundamental tone* **still further sound** *seven overtones.* If the higher harmonic **overtones** grow stronger and even overpower the fundamental tone, the sound grows shrill, but **when the discordant** overtones lying close together, higher than the tones just named, **overpower** the fundamental tone, the timbre becomes sharp and disagreeable. In bass **voices** which **use too** great an amount **of** breath, **the** overtones up to the sixteenth **are** sometimes heard, which gives such voices a harsh and disagreeable timbre. But **as the** tones of different voices have their harmonic overtones that properly belong to them, so every singing as well as every speaking voice has its characteristic timbre,—*i.e.* its peculiar ring by which we distinguish it from other voices.* Every voice has one, often two overtones, which predominate in every tone; and this it is that gives the voice its peculiar quality. This peculiarity is due to the particular form of the cavity of the mouth.

* The Voice in Singing.

CHAPTER II.

THE VOWELS.

THE vocal organ in man is a musical instrument, which is commonly compared with a so-called reed instrument as we see it in organ-pipes. The lungs are the bellows, the windpipe is the feeding-pipe, the larynx with the tone-generating vocal cords represents the reed instrument, and the cavity of the mouth the resonance-tube. Among all musical instruments, however, there is no one that, like the vocal organ of man, combines in itself the peculiarities of them all, no one that even approaches it in perfection, or is capable of such a vast and delicate variety of tones. But what distinguishes the organ of the human voice from all other instruments is the extraordinary rapidity and accuracy of its movements: not only do the vocal cords change their action and the degree of their tension with every different grade of tone, but all the parts of the cavity of the mouth put themselves in varying relations to one another with the slightest **change of** a sound. **As** every syllable which we utter consists **of several sounds, the** tuning of the cavity of **the mouth must, even for** the shortest syllable, change **several times. Of this** ceaseless activity **of the vocal instrument in speaking we** may easily satisfy ourselves by **simply observing the** movement **of the** lips and lower jaw of a person speaking, **and by** considering how much activity of the vocal organ this movement implies.

The **sounds we** make **in** speaking consist of **tones and noises. The** *noises* **and** characteristic tones **of the** speaking sounds, **as we** hear them in whispering, are formed **in** the **cavity of** the mouth, and are supported **in** speaking aloud **by** the *tones* of the larynx. **Speech** thus requires **a very com-**plicated mechanism, **as** it results *from the com-bined working* **of two very** *different actions* **of** our *vocal organs.*

About ten years ago, **Prof.** Helmholtz, in his "*Lehre von den Tonempfindungen,*" published **his** scientific investigations of the vowel sounds. **He** found, for instance, that **in** every vowel sound **the** cavity of the mouth is tuned to **a certain definite tone by** the changes of its several parts, **tongue,** lips, etc., and by the rise and fall of the larynx, and that this tone is wholly independent of age or sex, and is always the same, by whatever musical tone produced, or by whatever action of the vocal cords accompanied. What the cavity of the mouth in a child lacks in respect of room is supplied in **a** grown person by a greater closing of the aperture of the mouth, so that the resonance is the same in both cases. Only the different *shades* of the vowel, as pronounced **in** different dialects and languages, change the pitch **of** the peculiar characteristic tone of the vowel.*

Thus it makes no difference whether, for example, the vowel *o* be spoken with the note c or f. The tone with which the air in the mouth accords **will be the** same, **whether** it be a man or a child who **speaks it.**

* This tone is not an overtone, as it is universally represented. Even the most acute investigators have not hitherto regarded the voice in speaking in its true light, as the result of *two different actions working together.*

Though the vowel sounds in German are **susceptible** in pronunciation of but little change, yet **the** following tables indicate variations due **to the** different **localities in** which **the investigation of this subject has been pursued; but in English, where every vowel undergoes so many variations in pronunciation, it is hardly possible to fix the** precise pitch **of its** proper tone. This, however, is not important, the chief point **being** that **the** cavity **of the** mouth tunes itself for every vowel **to a** certain **fixed tone, which** gives it its characteristic clang.

The following **are the tones to which** the cavity **of the mouth** is tuned in the sounds of the different vowels as they have been ascertained **by** Helmholtz and Donders, **and** as they **are set down in** " *Die Lehre* **von den** *Tonempfindungen*." Therewith are given **also the** results **of** our investigations.

I. Helmholtz.

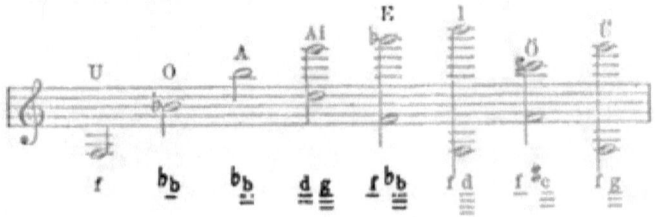

THE VOWELS. 27

II. Donders.

III. Seiler.

The results No. III. are given according to the American orchestra pitch, which is about half a tone higher than the European. Helmholtz says† that the **vowels** *u, o, a,* **have only one tone,** while the vowels *ai, e, i, ō, ü,* have **two** very distinct tones,‡ **and this is** explained by the fact **that in the case of the** latter vowels a sort of enclosure **is** formed in the cavity of the mouth, **dividing it into** two spaces, each of which **keeps** its own **pitch.** He compares this **form of the** cavity of the mouth **to a flask, the** neck of which corresponds with the

* I as it is spoken in the English word *ring.*
† *Lehre von den Tonempfindungen.*
‡ It should be constantly borne in mind by the reader that the examples given are taken from the German language.

tongue and lips in the front part of the mouth, and the body of it with the back part.*

Donders, as may be seen in the foregoing scale, gives for each vowel only one proper tone, and neither I nor my son was able, in the vowels *ai, e, i, ö, ü,* to distinguish the two tones claimed for them by Helmholtz, either by the unassisted ear or by the *resonators* expressly made for the purpose and consisting of two globes shaped like the cavity of the mouth as this disposes itself for *ai, e, i, ö,* and *ü*. As only the size, but not the form of a hollow globe, has influence upon the number of vibrations of its proper tone, so our *resonators*, connected with each other by a narrow opening, gave a tone corresponding to that of the two hol-

* In the investigation of these facts, Helmholtz made use of a row of tuning-forks and *resonators*. He held one after the other while sounding before his mouth, distinctly articulating the vowels. As soon as the cavity of the mouth was in accord with the vibrating tuning-fork, the latter began to sound more strongly; and so it was with the *resonators*. After he had thus found the proper tones of the vowels, he attempted to imitate the vowel sounds artificially, which he succeeded in doing tolerably plainly in the case of *a, o,* and *u,* but with the others only approximately, because the noises which accompany the vowel sounds could not be imitated.

low globes taken together; and not until the opening between the **two was** entirely closed—which, however, never happens in the cavity of the mouth when pronouncing the said vowel sounds—could each globe be set vibrating by itself.

To the **vowel *a*, as** in the German '*Vater*' or the English '*father*,' corresponds a funnel-shaped **form** of the cavity of the mouth, enlarging upward **from** the **larynx with** tolerable **regularity,** whereby **the** lips open **wide, the tip of the** tongue is lightly pressed against the lower teeth, and the root of the tongue is somewhat raised.

In uttering the vowel *e*, as in the German '*See*' or the English '*may*,' the lips are not so far apart as **in** the **case of** *a;* the opening of the mouth is more like a slit, as its corners are somewhat drawn **back;** the tip **of** the tongue presses against the **lower** teeth, and **the** body of the tongue against the roof **of** the mouth, in such a way, however, as to form a tubular opening between it and the tongue. The root of the tongue is drawn somewhat down, **so** that a second smaller space is made in the back of the mouth, which is connected with that in front by the tube-like opening we have just described.

In forming the vowel *i*, as **in the** German

'*Ring*' or the English '*ring*,' the slit-shaped opening of the mouth is narrower and longer than in *e;* the back of the tongue presses rather more broadly against the roof of the mouth, the **front space** of **the** cavity of the mouth becomes smaller **and the back space greater,** while the larynx is raised, and the tube-shaped **opening** between **the** tongue and the roof of the mouth is longer. In the case of the vowel *o,* as in the German or English '*So,*' the cavity of the mouth is narrowed **in** front by the lips, and **the** opening of the **mouth is round. The** tongue lies entirely flat, **and the root** of the tongue is drawn back against the palate, while the larynx is drawn downward **in order to** render the cavity of the mouth **as** spacious as possible. In making the **vowel *u*,** as in the German '*Hut*' or the English '*boot*,' **the mouth is less open** and less round than in *o,* the lips **are set** closer to the teeth, and **the** back part of the tongue touches the palate lightly, **so that** the air in the nasal cavity **is** made to **vibrate** in accord, which gives to the vowel *u* its peculiarly dull sound. The cavity of the mouth **is narrowest** in the case of *u*, and broadest in that of *a*.

The so-called *Umlaute*, in German, *ä*, *ö*, *ü*, as also the different shades of the vowels as they are made in the English language, are formed by a disposition of the mouth corresponding as closely as possible to that by which the vowels of which they are composed are formed. Thus, the tongue in *ä*, as in the German '*Bär*' or the English '*bear*,' has almost the same position as in *e:* that is, the same lowering of the tongue in its centre from the back towards the front; only, instead of the sides of the tongue pressing against the roof of the mouth, the tongue merely rises a little and allows the cavity of the mouth to be almost as broad as in the case of *a*. In the formation of *ö*, as in the German '*schön*,' and of *ü*, as in '*früh*,' the tongue keeps the same position as in *e* and *i*, while the cavity of the mouth is formed as for the *o* and *u*.

The diphthongs, such as *ei*, *ai*, *oi*, *au*, *ou*, etc., in which two vowels sound, one immediately after the other, require two different dispositions of the mouth, and accordingly each of their constituent vowels has its proper tone.

All vowel sounds are accompanied by noises, arising from the striking of the air upon the soft and hard parts of the interior of the mouth, and from the consequent rapid discords produced. Even before Helmholtz, Willis and Donders had discovered the characteristic tones of the vowels formed in the cavity of the mouth.

From the foregoing description it appears—first, that in speaking, the cavity of the mouth in the formation of every vowel adapts itself to an entirely distinct tone, which is the peculiar characteristic clang of that vowel; secondly, that these proper tones of the several vowels, made in the mouth, are wholly independent of the tones of the voice that come from the vocal cords vibrating in the larynx, and at every age and in both sexes are always the same; but the various shades given to the vowel sounds in the pronunciation of the different languages, and of different dialects of the same language, have, and they alone have, an influence upon their pitch.

The extent to which the larynx moves up and down in the forming of the vowels is about half an inch. Beginning with A in its natural position, it moves upward in E and I, downward in O and U, as they are pronounced in the previous examples.

THE VOWELS.

VOWELS.	HELMHOLTZ.	DONDERS.	SEILER.
U	f	f	f
O	♭b	d	♭a
A	♭b	♭b	♭d
Ö	f ♯e	g	♯f
Ü	f g	a	a
E	f ♭b	♯e	♭b
I	f d	f	♯f
Ai	d g	"	"

VOWELS.	WITH WORDS.	WILLIS.	HELMHOLTZ.
O	No	c	c
Ao	Nought	♭e	♭e
	Paw.	g	g
A	Part	♭d	♭d
	Paa	f	♭b
E	Pay	d	♭b
	Pet	e	e
I	See	g	d

CHAPTER III.

THE CONSONANTS.

WHILE so much has been accomplished by recent investigations in the domain of Acoustics in respect to the formation of the vowel sounds, as we have shown in the foregoing pages, little or nothing, on the other hand, is to be found in scientific works on the subject of the musical character of the Consonants.

Helmholtz remarks, in passing, that the consonants *m*, *n*, and *f* have overtones: beyond this brief observation, the consonants are almost universally treated as mere noises. It is only necessary, however, to use the whispering voice to be satisfied that, with their characteristic noises, most of the consonants have also a distinct musical clang.

These proper tones are distinguished from those of the vowels by the fact that difference of language or of dialect has no effect in changing their pitch, which is always the same in the speaking voice of man, in all conditions,—that is, so long as the consonant is spoken alone without any connection with other sounds of speech. One may easily satisfy himself of the fact by requesting several individuals to sound a consonant, *b, f,* or *s,* for example, and endeavor to change its pitch. They will not be able to make the sound higher or lower than the rest. Thus, in setting the key-note of a song, instead of giving the note with a tuning-fork or whistle, one who knows the proper tone of a consonant has only to whisper that consonant to be able to give the key-note quite correctly. Only when the consonants *g, k, d, t,* and *f* are uttered in connection with such sounds of speech as have a higher pitch than their own do their proper tones seem to sound higher, but this only to a certain limit. In the word *Stick,* for instance, the proper tone of the *t,* placed as it is between *s* and *i,* the proper tones of which are much higher than its own, appears to be higher than in the word *to,* or than when it is uttered by itself; and this is probably because the cavity of the mouth in such rapid utterance cannot accurately enough accommodate itself to a lower tone standing between two higher ones.

Dr. Wolf places the limit of the highest pitch of all self-sounding consonants, spoken in connection with higher sounds of speech, a whole octave above that of their individual proper tone. But the results of our most careful investigations do not go beyond a fifth or sixth.

Most of those who have written upon Speech have invented names and divisions for the different classes of sounds made in speaking. Dr. Wolf arranges the consonants according to their musical character into four groups, which I shall adopt, and which are as follows:

I. The simple self-sounding consonants, which can be sounded purely and independently of the vowels. These are *r*, hard *ch*, *b*, *p*, *g*, *k*, *d*, *t*, *f*, *v*, *s*, and the soft *g* and *ch*.

II. The compound self-sounding consonants, such as *sch*, *x*, *z*.

III. The simple tone-borrowing consonants, which borrow their musical sound from a vowel sound and are distinctly audible only in connection with it, as *h*, *l*, *m*, *n*.

IV. The compound tone-borrowing consonant, which is the *w*.

In the formation of all **the** consonants there **is** found somewhere in the cavity **of** the mouth an **enclosure** or **narrower** space, **against and** through which the exhaled breath presses, and so is **produced a** distinct noise quite independent **of their** musical proper tone. The pitch of the musical tone which accompanies this noise is dependent upon the size **of** the resonant space in the cavity of the mouth, **which space is largest in** *b* **and** *p* **and smallest in** *s*.

I. The Simple Self-sounding Consonants.

THE *B* AND *P* SOUNDS.

To form the *b* **sound** the lips are **first** firmly **closed, and** the breath, compressed as much as possible, **is** forced against them. The lips then parting by a rapid movement, the confined air escapes **with** a sudden puff, like **a** miniature explosion.

Given the same disposition **of** the mouth and the **action** just described for **the** formation of the *b* sound, only executed with more force and energy, and we have the *p* sound, the proper tone **of** both these consonants being very nearly one and the same; at the most the pitch of *p* is the higher by something more than **half a** tone.

The tone to which in *b* the air in the cavity of the mouth is tuned has 320 vibrations in a second, and comes nearest to the note e with 323½ vibrations (natural pitch). The *p* has 346 vibrations, and comes near to the f with 344½ vibrations.

When the disposition of the mouth for **the formation** of the **sound** *b* **is kept** unchanged, **one may** easily satisfy himself in regard to its **pitch** by snapping the finger against the cheek. One may also by the same means distinguish the proper tones of the vowels. For most **of the** consonants, however, the cavity **of** the mouth **is** too small to allow their **proper tones to be** heard in this manner.

THE *G* AND *K* SOUNDS.

The part played by the lips in the formation of *b* and *p* as above described, in the case of *g* and *k* devolves upon the body of the tongue;

THE CONSONANTS.

these sounds being formed by its pressure against the roof of the mouth and quick withdrawal from it, the point of impact being found more or less **farther back in** the mouth as the modes of speaking vary with different peoples and in different languages, without any influence on the pitch of its proper tone. **As in the case of** p **as compared with** b, **the** k **has a** higher pitch than g **by** something more than half a tone, which is due to the greater force required in its formation. The proper tone of g has 576 vibrations, and comes nearest to the note $\underline{\underline{d}}$, which has 582; while k has 616, nearest to $\flat\underline{\underline{e}}$ with $614\frac{1}{2}$ vibrations.

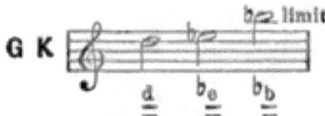

THE D AND T SOUNDS.

As with b and p it is the lips and with g and k the body of the tongue that are brought into requisition, so in the case of d and t it is the tip of the tongue that makes the enclosure, by first pressing against the upper front teeth and then quickly withdrawing with a snap, thus letting the confined air escape, both the lips and the upper and lower teeth being slightly parted. Their proper tones are likewise almost the same, that of *t* being the higher by about half a tone, and for the same reason as before given.

The proper tone of *d* has 720 vibrations, and lies nearest to ♯f, which has 726, while *t* has 768, lying nearest to g with 776 vibrations.

The six consonants described above are all formed in precisely the same way, by the pressure and sudden withdrawal of the lips, by the body and by the tip of the tongue.

THE *V* AND *F* SOUNDS.

These sounds are made when the under lip, pressed against the front upper teeth, forms with the upper lip in the middle of the mouth a small opening, on the edges of which the stream of breath, inhaled or exhaled, breaks and is set

THE CONSONANTS.   41

vibrating. The air pressing through this little opening forms the sound of *f*. By a weaker expulsion of the air there is produced the German *v*. The difference between these two sounds depends only upon the stronger or weaker impulse given to the breath. The noise, however, accompanying the *f* is attended by a greater number of high inharmonic overtones, which are formed at the opening of the mouth. The pitch of *f* with 862 vibrations is like the a̲ of the natural pitch with 864 vibrations.

THE *S* SOUND.

Like the *f*, the *s* is formed by the emission of the breath. While the tongue lies near to the lower teeth and the lips are parted, the air is driven between the upper and lower teeth. As the tongue thereby is somewhat raised, and the upper and lower teeth are brought together, there remains for the sound of *s* in the cavity of the mouth only a very narrow space, whence it naturally follows that the pitch of this consonant is very high. By a gentle emission of the air the sound of *s* has 3700 vibrations, being nearest to ♭b with 3666 vibrations.

THE SOFT *G* AND *CH* SOUNDS.

These sounds, as they are given in German after *e* and *i*, do not occur in the English language. They are likewise formed by expelling the compressed air through a narrow passage formed by the pressure of the tongue against the roof of the mouth, in such a manner that the middle of the tongue is lowered from the back towards the front, and a narrow, pipe-shaped opening is formed for the passing air. In forming these narrow passages the points of impact are different in different persons and countries, being more or less forward in the mouth. The cavity of the mouth has in the soft *g* and *ch* the same pitch as the vowel *i*, namely, the d with 2328 vibrations.

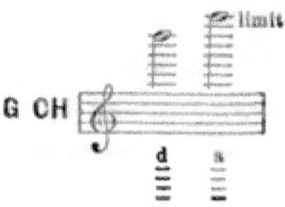

The hard *ch*, as in the German words *machen*, *lachen*, etc., is formed by pressing the root of the tongue against the roof of the mouth, expelling the breath at the same time; thus very differently from the soft *ch* in the words *Bäche*, *ich*, *glücklich*, etc. If the quick movement which the root of the tongue makes in forming the *ch* be made energetically and very far back in the mouth, the palate is set vibrating by the impulse of a stronger stream of air, and there instantly comes the sound of *r* as it is heard in the North of Germany and in English. This is the so-called uvular or palatal *r*. The proper tone of the hard *ch* is the same as that of the palatal *r*. Its pitch will be given hereafter when we come to speak of the latter. The above-described manner of forming the hard *ch* as well as the palatal *r*, inasmuch as it takes place so far back in the mouth, is very unfavorable to a good development of the speaking voice, and especially, as we shall see by-and-by, to its reach. In English the hard *ch* does not occur, and it is certainly for all English-speaking persons who are learning to speak German the most difficult to imitate correctly.

I have often been asked why German dramatic artists pronounce the hard *ch* as if it were equivalent to the English *sh*, and I have found that precisely those among our German actors who use the vocal organ in the most correct and beautiful way, in the endeavor to give more reach to this unfavorable sound, form it unconsciously farther forward in the mouth, where the position and pitch of the cavity of the mouth are such as to produce the *sh*.

THE *R* SOUND. THE LINGUAL *R*.

As the uvular *r* is produced by the vibrations of the uvula, so the lingual *r* is formed by the vibrations of the tip of the tongue. When the tongue is allowed to be in the same position in which the sound of *d* is produced, and the tip of the tongue is raised and set vibrating by the breath, we can distinguish in the rattling, intermitting sound of *r* certain other very low sounds. According to Wolf, in the uvular *r* the low c̿ with 16½ vibrations is produced most **strongly**. In the lingual *r* comes the C with 33 vibrations.

With these lowest tones̄ he found several overtones, of which he distinguishes the C with 129 vibrations as the proper tone of the *r*. The lowest tone mentioned by Wolf the ear cannot distinctly perceive. According to our investigations, the C with 64 vibrations is the proper tone of the lingual *r;* and for the uvular *r*, D with 72½ vibrations.

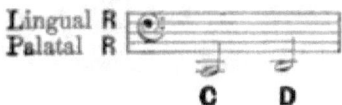

II. The Compound Self-sounding Consonants.

THE GERMAN *SCH* OR ENGLISH *SH*.

In the formation of the *sch* (*sh*) the vocal apparatus is adapted at one and the same moment to the utterance of two different consonants. There are created in the mouth two narrow passages through which the air is expelled: the one like that which is made forward in the mouth for *s*, the other as in forming the German hard *ch*, the root of the tongue being pressed against the roof of the mouth, and its edges lying round in contact with the teeth, while the centre is raised, so that the resonance-space between the two passages is enlarged. It is evident that by the breaking of the stream of air at two different places two different sounds are made; but, as one can in a flute clearly distinguish two tones, one of which, the flute-tone, is produced in the hollow space of the instrument by the vibrations of the air, the other by the breaking of the stream of air on the sharp edges of the aperture, so in pronouncing the *sch* what one hears is in reality three tones,—the $\bar{\bar{d}}$ formed in the cavity of the mouth, the $\underset{=}{\flat b}$ formed by the breaking of the air on the teeth, and a third resultant tone, which is produced in the air by the other two sounding together, and which is the f. The $\bar{\bar{d}}$ has 2328 vibrations, the $\underset{=}{\flat b}$ 3666, and the f $\bar{\bar{1378}}$. This third tone is often so prominent that one hears very clearly the fourth sixth chord of B♭ major.

THE CONSONANTS. 47

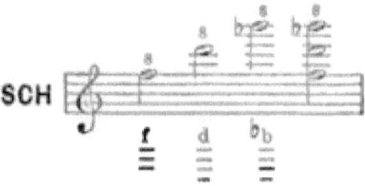

A stronger expulsion of the breath in uttering the *sh* causes the vowel *i* to be heard quite plainly sounding with it, because the pitch of the **cavity of the mouth is the same as** that of this **vowel.** The English *ch* is composed of the sounds of *t* and *sh*.

In the English *th*, **which is** composed of two sounds, of **which one** is produced by **the** striking **and** the other by the friction of the air,—*i.e.*, the *t* and **a** sound similar **to** the *s*,—the cavity of the mouth is tuned to the proper tone of the sound of *t;* **for,** instead of the tip **of** the tongue **lying, as in the** *s*, near the lower teeth **so that the** breath can **pass unimpeded between,** in forming *th* it continues, after bringing **out** by a sudden stroke the sound of *t* to be raised **in** the same place, **and thus** forms **a** narrow passage through which the expelled air must pass before **it** presses through the narrow slits between the teeth.

The German *z* **and** *x* are likewise two compound sounds, which, however, are heard one after the other in rapid succession, of which one is produced by the striking and the other by the friction of the air. In the *z*, *s* follows *t;* in the *x*, *s* follows *k*, the proper tones of which have already been given.

III. The Simple Tone-borrowing Consonants.

THE *H*.

H has no proper musical tone, and can be heard only in connection with a vowel. The Greeks did not hold *h* to be a consonant. In its formation there is nowhere in the mouth any enclosure, or, indeed, any obstacle to the passage of the breath, producing the noises by which the other consonants are accompanied. The *h* is thus nothing more than the breath itself more vigorously expelled and driven along the walls of the mouth and the cavity of the larynx, as is the case when the action of the lungs is increased by running or fast walking.

THE *L*.

L is formed, like *d*, with the tip of the tongue; but, while in *d* the point of the tongue is put in contact with the upper teeth and the roof of the mouth and then suddenly withdrawn, allowing the compressed air to escape, in *l* the tongue slowly touches the same places forward in the mouth, and allows the breath to flow quietly out, only slightly kept back. The air thus detained divides and streams out on both sides of the tongue along the cheeks towards the opening of the mouth. *L*, like *h*, has no proper tone, which is evident from the slow movement of the tongue and the division of the stream of air. So soon, however, as any tone sounds with it the *l* sounds also, and, although the cavity of the mouth is not in accord with any proper tone, one hears a tone similar to that of the vowel *i*, often entirely concealing the *l*. This peculiarity of the *l* may be the reason why it is often considered as a semi-vowel. According to Valentin, the Romanic languages appear to regard *l* in this light, often using *i* in place of it: as, for example, *planus* (Latin), *piano* (Italian), *flos* (Latin), *fiore* (Italian), etc.

THE *M* AND *N*.

These two so-called resonants are in their formation very much alike. According to Czermak's investigations of the utterance of the vowels, the palate is so raised that no air, or only a very little, can pass out through the **nose**. In the utterance of *m* and *n*, on the contrary, the palate is so placed that the larger portion of the breath passes through the nose. The resonance, then, for these **sounds** is mostly **in the space above the soft** palate. *M* and *n* **have** no audible **tone** of their own, and can be considered only **as**, so to speak, grace-notes before or after the tone of the vowel. They cannot be used in connection with consonants, because they are heard distinctly only when joined to vowels. Neither have they, like the other consonants, any independent characteristic noises: they depend entirely upon their resonance. When **one** attempts with **the** whispering voice, that is, without the help of the tones of the larynx, to pronounce *m* and *n*, only a sort of audible breath **is** perceived, generated by the friction of **the air in** the nasal cavities. In forming these sounds, the way for the air through the mouth is entirely **closed, and opens** only through the nose. The *m* **is formed when,** as in the case of *b*, the lips are shut, and instead of allowing the compressed breath, by a sudden motion, to escape, the lips **are kept** closed and the air passes out through the nose. When, on the other hand, having the mouth in the same position as in forming *d*, the enclosure in the mouth is formed by the tip of the tongue pressed against the upper teeth, there is produced the sound of *n*. According to Helmholtz, through the changing position of the soft palate a larger quantity of air passes through the nose in the formation of *m*, and a less in that of *n*. A marked difference between *m* and *n* is perceived only when a vowel sounds before or after them.

IV. The Compound Tone-borrowing Consonant.

The sound of *w* in German is, according to Brücke, the mingling of a consonant and a vowel. The German *w*, like *m* and *n*, cannot be heard without an audible vowel sound. When it is uttered audibly there is heard a weak sound of *w*. Let the mouth take the same position as in the formation of *f*, and let the sound, shorter and weaker, be joined at the same time with the vowel *u*, the mouth being quietly opened wide, and we have the German *w*. The English *w* (double *u*) is a sound between the pure *u* and the German *w*; it is heard when one begins to sound the vowel *u* and then gradually contracts the cavity of the mouth.

52   THE VOICE IN SPEAKING.

A TABULAR STATEMENT OF THE PITCH OF THE SELF-SOUNDING SPEAKING SOUNDS.

THE CONSONANTS. 53

Although it is attempted in the foregoing table to give the pitch of the several proper tones of our speaking sounds as accurately as possible, this is not, however, I conceive, essential. The main point is this: *That most of the consonants, as well as all the vowels, have distinct tones of their own, characteristic of each, to which the cavity of the mouth is tuned, as we have shown; and, furthermore, that these proper tones of the speaking sounds, independently of age and sex, keep approximately the same pitch in the speech of all human beings.* Consonants are not, therefore, as has hitherto been assumed, indefinite noises. As with the vowels, the main fact is the proper tone of the sound forming in the cavity of the mouth; the larger portion of the air is employed in the formation of this proper musical tone with its regular vibrations, and only the lesser portion breaks upon the obstacles which it meets, thus becoming *noise* with irregular vibrations and dissonant overtones.

The tone in the cavity of the mouth gives to the vowels their characteristic timbre, and is more prominent and perceptible than their accompanying noises. But the consonants derive their peculiar character from their noises, which are so prominent that their proper tones have hitherto escaped observation. Differ ever so much as nations may in speech, still, vowels and consonants ever alternate, the one with the other, and indeed mostly in such a way that the cavity of the mouth is not forced to too great a change in its tuning. Thus they mutually relieve one another, so that the speaking organs are less fatigued, and with the same impulse of breath are able to produce a great many different sounds.

The words which we put into sentences in speaking are composed of syllables. A syllable consists of one vowel sound, or two vowel sounds immediately following each other, and one or more consonants. The vowels require for their characteristic tones a larger space in the mouth than the consonants, and while the mouth is tuned and untuned for the vowel sound of a syllable, the parts of the mouth on their way forward and backward form the consonants belonging to the syllable. In other words, a syllable is a group of speaking sounds produced by one pulse of breath, with various quickly succeeding movements of the speaking mechanism, the mouth opening and closing for the tuning or untuning of the vowel. It is on this account difficult to pronounce two consonants, similarly formed, coming close together in the same syllable, as, for instance, *d* and *k*, and impossible to form double consonants in the same syllables, as *tt, pp;* but it instantly becomes easy when they are separated by a vowel, as *tat, pep,* etc.

When, for example, the syllable *run* is pronounced, the tip of the tongue, while the cavity of the mouth sets itself in tune for the *u*, forms the *r;* and as it untunes itself the mouth closes with the *n*, with which the syllable is ended. And for the speaking of another syllable there is required a new opening of the mouth and a new pulse of the breath.

In looking over the proper tones of the sounds in speech, we find that the lowest, the tone of *r*, the C 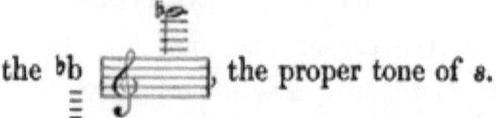, is separated full six octaves from the ♭b , the proper tone of *s*.

When one considers the vast compass in which the proper tones of the speaking sounds range, in reference to the manifold movements made in forming the noises which accompany them, and the rapidity and certainty with which all these variations of activities are carried on, the vast capability of the speaking organ seems hardly conceivable. There is certainly no artificial instrument that approaches it in this respect. And the greatest artist, if such an instrument were put into his hands, would be utterly unable to overcome the difficulties which we in speaking unconsciously make light of every day.

The whispering voice, with which we are able to make ourselves heard within narrow limits, consists merely of the tones and noises of the cavity of the mouth made with a quiet flow of the breath. *Only in speaking aloud* are these tones and noises supported by the tones produced by the vibrating vocal cords in the larynx, and which give to speech fulness, melody, and reach. *Our common speaking, therefore, is to be regarded as the result of the combined action of two different instruments,* which also act separately; the tones and noises made in the cavity of the mouth alone, that is, the *speaking sounds*, as in the whispering voice, are made by one of these instruments, and the *musical* *tones* of the vocal cords, as in singing without words, by the other.* In speaking aloud, and in singing with words, both instruments

* It has recently been proved by several cases that distinct, although soft and low, speaking is possible even when the larynx is closed so that no breath passes through it. The air contained in the mouth alone can be applied to the production of speech when no assistance can be had from the larynx. Through the kindness of Prof. Störk, of Vienna, my son was made acquainted with a case in point. A patient in the insane-asylum in that city cut her throat and wounded the vocal cords, which, in healing, grew together so that she could not breathe, and it was necessary to introduce a small tube into the windpipe below the larynx to keep her from suffocating. After some months she began to speak, and yet no opening of the glottis could be discovered with the laryngoscope. The opinion of Prof. Störk, that the patient was enabled to speak, by means of the air in the mouth and nasal cavities alone, was opposed by many of his colleagues, who insisted that there must be some opening between the vocal cords. In a second attempt the patient succeeded in killing herself, and a post-mortem examination revealed the fact that the vocal cords had so grown together that neither water nor air could pass through them. At the suggestion of Prof. Störk, a young man undertook to practise in speaking with a closed glottis, and, to make sure that no air was allowed to pass through it before speaking in the above-mentioned way, he inhaled the smoke

are employed. All the characteristic tones and noises of our speaking sounds, as they are formed in the mouth and shown in the whispering voice, become, when spoken aloud, supported and strength-

of a cigarette. The closest observation could not detect any escape of the smoke thus inhaled.

Prof. Valentin and Dr. Wolf also mention each a case in which, in consequence of unsuccessful attempts at suicide, the glottis had so grown together that the breathing had to be through a small silver tube, which was introduced between the two uppermost rings of the windpipe. As soon as this little tube was closed by the finger, instantly there came a fit of suffocation. In both cases the sufferers learned by degrees to make themselves understood, although only in a whisper. The sounds that they made most distinctly were $b, p, g, k, f, d, t, s, sch$. The vowels were more difficult, and could be uttered only in connection with other sounds, and it was the same with m, n, h, l, r. These last were difficult, because the air in the mouth, not being increased by the breath from the lungs, did not suffice for their formation. Of the vowels, t was the easiest.

Speaking is also possible even without the tongue, for there are cases on record in which the whole of the tongue had been removed by a surgical operation, and still the patients were able to articulate, with the exception of those consonants which are produced by the tip of the tongue.*

* Tongue not Essential to Speech, by Twisleton, London.

ened by musical tones. These musical tones, according to their own laws, are produced with great rapidity and certainty by the vocal cords in the larynx. And to them we give in speaking a certain musical arrangement, according to the emotion for which we seek expression.

Musical tones have thus their own instrument, different from that of the speaking sounds as shown in the whispering voice; and the action of this instrument will be described in the following chapter.

It is here for the first time that this path has been trodden in the study of the speaking voice, by which the fact is arrived at that it is the combined result of two wholly different actions of our vocal organs. That hitherto in all the investigations of this subject, sounds of Speech as heard in the whispering voice have never been separated from the vocal tones, and that the two actions, so very different from each other, have been studied together and considered only as one, is owing, I suppose, to the fact that it is but recently that Science has turned its attention in this direction at all. Up to this hour, in all that has been written on the subject, the voice has been treated almost exclusively from the æsthetic side: that is, expression in speaking has mostly been considered, while the physiology of the voice, owing to the obscurity in which the subject was involved, has been almost entirely neglected.

My son, Dr. Carl Seiler, has rendered me great assistance both in determining the proper tones of speaking sounds as given in the foregoing pages and in executing the drawings for this book.

CHAPTER IV.

THE VOCAL TONES.

THE laryngoscope was hardly invented before it came to be widely known and used; and many persons, without the necessary musical or scientific qualifications therefor, have undertaken to observe with it the mechanism whereby tones are produced in the larynx. Many results of such superficial observations have been published even as new discoveries, and systems of teaching have been founded thereon.*

* A physician who handled the laryngoscope with great skill affirmed that the mechanism in the larynx was the same for all the registers of the voice, and a singing teacher instantly published a manual based upon this strange assertion. As a proof of the correctness thereof, they sang to me the scale up and down, and really succeeded in singing within the compass of two octaves, with the second chest-register. The gentlemen did not appear to be aware that these unnaturally produced tones were wholly devoid of musical character.

Every one who in any department of science seeks with an honest zeal for truth knows how such inexactly observed facts, instead of promoting knowledge, always hinder its progress. On this account, it is proper that I should briefly state the way in which I have investigated the vocal tones and the mode of their production.

When I proposed to myself to study more carefully the mechanism of the human voice, it did not escape my attention that the tones of one and the same voice are divided into groups, the peculiar timbre of which shows a more or less observable difference. But before I permitted myself to attempt, by the help of the laryngoscope, to seek for the cause of this fact, I considered it indispensably necessary first to know what was to be understood by a perfectly correct natural tone of voice, and also to learn to sing such tones. By the kindness of Prof. Helmholtz, I became acquainted with the physical conditions upon which pure musical tones depend, and, after long-continued practice, I succeeded in producing such tones and in making them habitual. Not until I had prepared myself by years of faithful study, and knew the several physical sensations accompanying a perfectly natural musical tone in the different groups, did I begin to observe in myself, with the laryngoscope, the movements in the larynx during the production of tones. In order to draw correct conclusions from such observation, attention must be specially directed to the physical sensations which, in a correct position of the mouth, accompany the formation of a perfect musical tone. For, in using the laryngoscope, the mouth must be opened very wide, and all its parts be so drawn aside and so posed that a full view of the glottis shall be afforded. As in this way the resonance and reflexion in the cavity of the mouth become disturbed, it is not possible to distinguish the different groups of tones by their timbre alone. When I succeeded at last in obtaining such command of the parts of the mouth that I could see the whole glottis, I always found the same movements in the formation of the same tones, changing and returning in the same manner. I then sought to make like observation in others, and selected for the purpose persons who never had had any instruction in singing, and whose voices were consequently entirely natural. Professional singers, or such as had received instruction in singing as

THE VOCAL TONES.

it is commonly given, I found for the most part to be wholly unfit for the desired observation. For, with a few distinguished exceptions, the voices of such singers are so artificially vitiated that they are no longer in a natural normal condition. The results of the observation of such voices would belong to the class of *facts inexactly observed*, from which every honest inquirer cannot keep too far aloof.*

The larynx is the funnel-shaped termination of the windpipe, widening upwards. It consists of differently-shaped cartilages, more or less movable, ligaments, and muscles. The case of the larynx consists of the thyroid cartilage (*a*) and the cricoid cartilage (*b*), as the following drawing of a larynx (Fig. I.), somewhat reduced, shows. The interior of the larynx consists of the arytenoid cartilages, the cartilages of Wrisberg, the two pairs of vocal cords, the cartilages of Santorini, and the cuneiform cartilages.

The cuneiform cartilages reach from the vocal

---

* In The Voice in **Singing, the** laryngoscope, as well **as** the way in which it is **to be used,** is described, and what **is** stated there need not be repeated here, since this method **of observation** is generally **known.**

process of the arytenoid cartilage, within the edges of the vocal cords, half the length of the same.

Fig. I.—The Larynx.

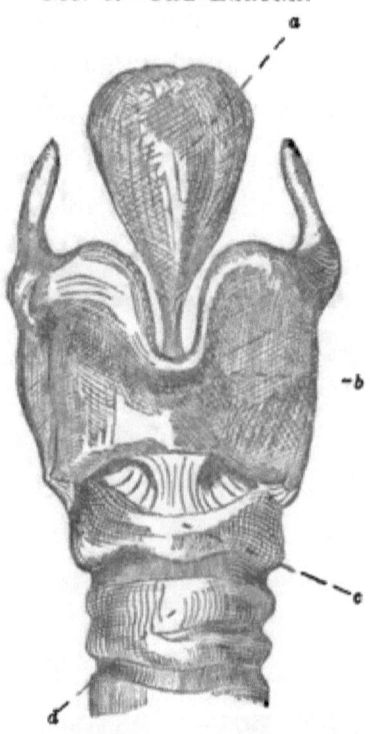

a. Epiglottis. *b.* Thyroid Cartilage. *c.* Cricoid Cartilage. *d.* Trachea.

In the drawing (Fig. III.) we see,* stretched from the anterior surface of the arytenoid cartilages extending towards the centre of the inner wall of

---

* The Voice in Singing (Appendix).

the thyroid cartilage, the two pairs of cords, consisting of folds of the mucous membrane which

Fig. II.—The Interior of the Larynx in Quiet Breathing and in Whispering.

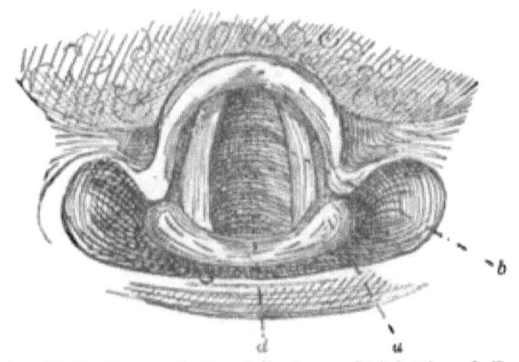

a. Arytenoid Cartilages. b. Vocal Cords. c. Epiglottis. d. Trachea.

Fig. III.—The Interior of the Larynx in the Formation of Tones in Speaking Aloud.

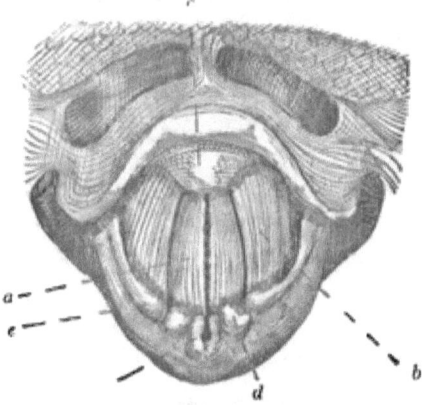

a. Vocal Cords. b. False Vocal Cords. c. Epiglottis. d. Arytenoid Cartilages. e. Wrisberg Cartilages.

lines the whole larynx. The two lower of these cords (*a, a,* Figs. II., III.), the vocal cords strictly so called, into which the cuneiform cartilages project, have their points of attachment at the arytenoid cartilages, somewhat lower than the upper pair.

Each of these parallel pairs of cords forms, between their edges, a slit running antero-posteriorly. The lower, or true vocal cords, approach in vocalization to close contact, while the upper cords scarcely move, and leave a wide elliptical opening between them. As the upper cords have their points of attachment posteriorly and higher, they form with the lower cords two lateral cavities, the ventricles. The two pairs of cords, therefore, are the free interior edges of the membrane lining the whole larynx, and extending into it to the right and left.

Only the lower vocal cords serve directly for the generation of sound. More or less stretched, and presenting resistance to the air forcibly expelled from the lungs through the trachea, they are thus made to vibrate. The upper or false vocal cords do not co-operate with them to generate tone, but, like all the remaining parts of the mouth and

THE VOCAL TONES.   69

throat, belong to the resonance apparatus of the voice, to which also appertains the back part of the mouth, the pharynx, above the œsophagus, *i.e.*, the throat or gullet. This is separated from the anterior cavity of the mouth by the soft palate, the form and place of which in the mouth every one knows.*

When a normal voice utters its lowest tones

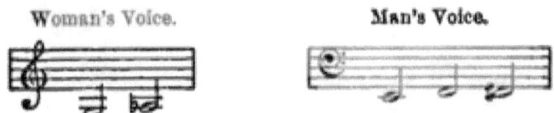

upon the vowel *ä*, as it is pronounced in the German word *Bär* (English *bear*),—this being the vowel sound most favorable for observation,—the following may be observed in the mirror:

The arytenoid cartilages, with great rapidity, raise their points, the cartilages of Santorini,

---

* The reader, if particularly interested in the anatomy of the vocal organ, is referred for a more minute description of it to the Appendix to The Voice in Singing, and to any Manual of Anatomy. I have given above only what is necessary in treating of the character of those parts of the larynx which co-operate in the formation of sound.

in their mucous membranous covering, and close firmly together, as is shown in Fig. III. In like manner, with equal swiftness, the vocal cords approach each other, until their edges touch through their entire length. The upper, or false vocal cords, likewise approach each other, leaving, however, as may be seen in the drawing, a relatively wide, elliptically-shaped space between them.

When the scale is slowly sung upward legato, step by step, the above-described movement of the arytenoid cartilages and the vocal cords is repeated with every new tone, partly separating and quickly closing again. The vocal cords, in the production of the lowest tones of the voice, are moved through their whole length and breadth by large, loose vibrations, which are communicated also to the other parts of the interior of the larynx.

With every higher tone the glottis* is somewhat shortened, and the vocal cords are more and more stretched. The raising of the pitch is thus effected by the greater stretching and shortening to a certain point.

---

* The glottis is the narrow slit between the two vocal cords and the arytenoid cartilages.

THE VOCAL TONES. 71

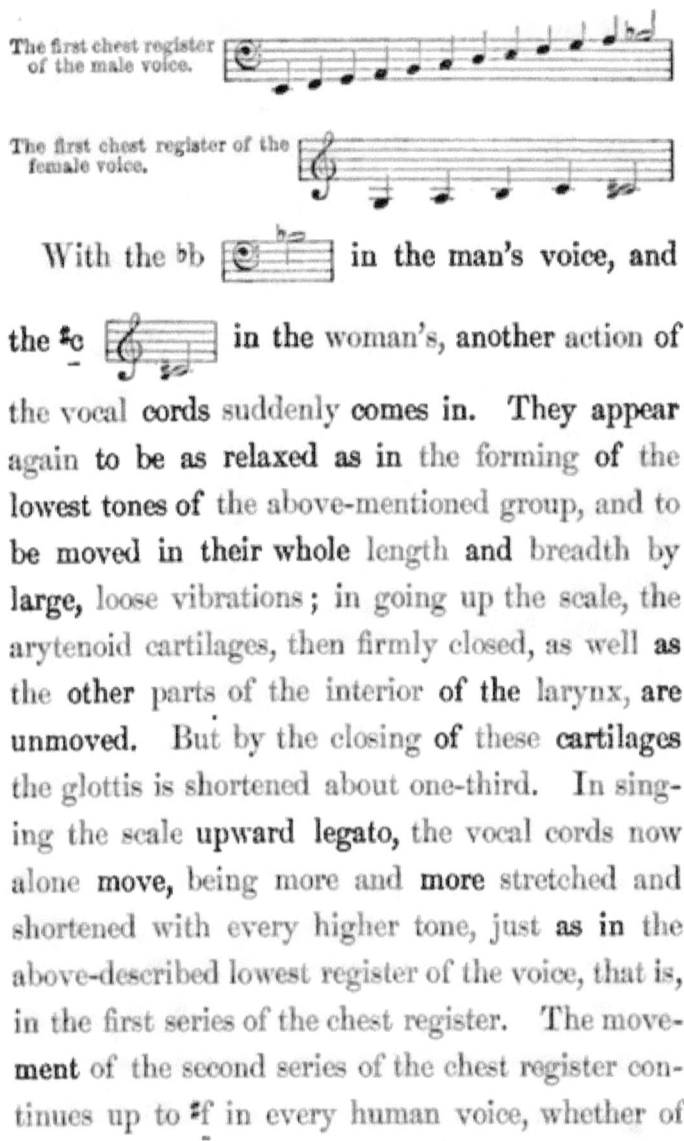

With the ♭♭ [notation] in the man's voice, and the ♯c [notation] in the woman's, another action of the vocal cords suddenly comes in. They appear again to be as relaxed as in the forming of the lowest tones of the above-mentioned group, and to be moved in their whole length and breadth by large, loose vibrations; in going up the scale, the arytenoid cartilages, then firmly closed, as well as the other parts of the interior of the larynx, are unmoved. But by the closing of these cartilages the glottis is shortened about one-third. In singing the scale upward legato, the vocal cords now alone move, being more and more stretched and shortened with every higher tone, just as in the above-described lowest register of the voice, that is, in the first series of the chest register. The movement of the second series of the chest register continues up to ♯f in every human voice, whether of man, woman, or child. This ♯f is the point of transition from the chest tones to the falsetto tones.

Second chest register of man's voice.

Second chest register of women and children.

That this ♯f is the natural point of transition, in all voices, from the chest voice to the falsetto, was known to the old Italian singing masters; for the a , by which instruments are usually tuned, and which was regarded by them as the highest chest tone, had, two hundred and fifty years ago, 370 vibrations, the same number as our present ♯f.

With the rise and development of instrumental music, the orchestra pitch has steadily but quite imperceptibly risen higher and higher, as stringed instruments sound more beautifully when higher tuned. In the year 1700, the a had 410 vibrations, and to-day, here in America, from 450 to 458, in Germany and France 435, *i.e.*, just half a tone lower than in this country. But as, while the pitch has thus been rising, human voices continue the same, it is very natural that a can no longer be sung with the chest register, as was the rule in former times, lying as it now does so far above the natural limit of the chest register. As soon as, in singing the scale upward, the ♯f is passed, instantly with the g the glottis again takes part in its whole length.

While, however, in the production of the tones of the two chest registers the vocal cords are seen to be moved by large, loose vibrations through their whole length and breadth, when the voice enters the falsetto register, only their fine inner edges are seen to be vibrating. While the arytenoid cartilages separate and quickly close with every new tone, higher or lower, of this group, just as in the case of the lowest series of the chest register, the vocal cords shorten with every higher gradation of tone, and show greater tension up to the ♭e in man's voice and to the ♯c in woman's.

At these points of the scale the arytenoid cartilages are instantly firmly closed again, whereby the glottis appears shortened a third, as in the transition from the first to the second chest register. The vocal cords again relax their tension just as suddenly, only their fine inner edges vibrating, as in the first falsetto register, and as in the other registers, shortening and stretching more and more with every higher gradation of tone to ♯f, at which tone the head voice in women and children begins.

Second Falsetto Register.   Woman's Voice.

The second falsetto register of man's voice is commonly thin, and is very rarely used. The head tones belong almost exclusively to women and children, and are found only very rarely in men's voices. The head voice embraces five to ten tones, and comes from a repeated partial closing of the glottis. The fine elastic pair of cartilages, the cuneiform cartilages, which are hidden within the mucous membrane of the vocal cords, extend from the arytenoid cartilages half the length of the vocal cords. In the head tones they close firmly together with the arytenoid cartilages, just as the arytenoid cartilages do in the

FIG. IV.—THE INTERIOR OF THE LARYNX GIVING THE HEAD TONES.

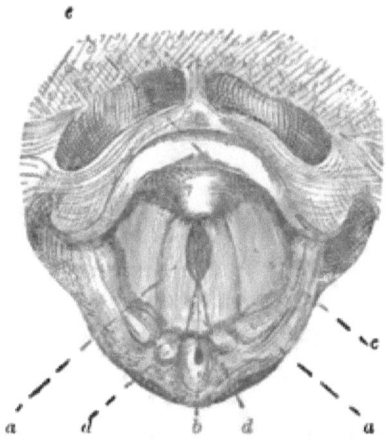

a. Vocal Cords.   *b.* Arytenoid Cartilage.   *c.* False Vocal Cords.
d. Cuneiform Cartilage.   *e.* Epiglottis.

first chest and the first falsetto register. Hence there appears, forward, directly under the epiglottis, an oval opening, which with every higher tone grows smaller and rounder, and the fine vibrating edges of which produce the highest tones of the voice as seen in Fig. IV.

These two registers, the second falsetto and the head register, are not used in speaking even by women, but only by little children. The movements of the vocal cords above described, in the different groups of tones or registers, always change at the same tone of the scale in all men's voices, whether the voice be deep or high. The transition from the first to the second chest register in man's voice is at ♭b [musical notation], and in woman's voice at ♯c [musical notation], whether it be a soprano or an alto. The difference in voices lies only in the greater fulness and beauty of the higher or lower registers, which registers usually are the easiest and most natural.

THE VOCAL TONES.

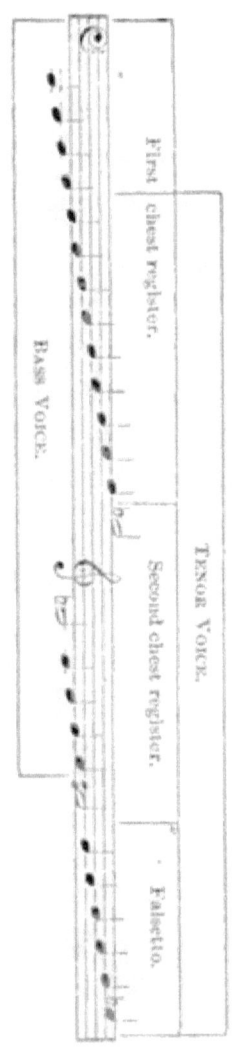

MAN'S VOICE.

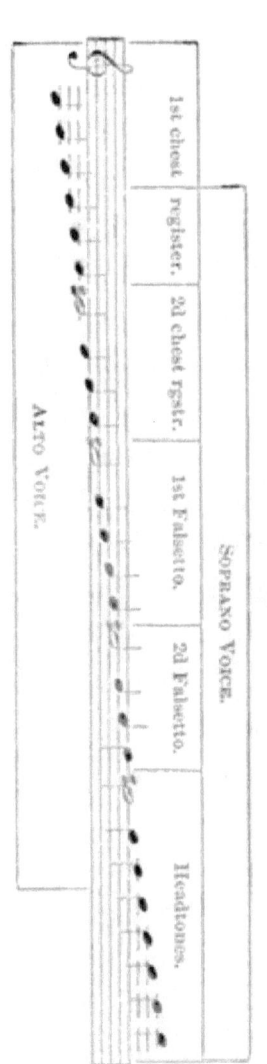

WOMAN'S VOICE.

As soon as it is attempted to transcend these natural limits of the registers in singing the ascending scale with the same action in the larynx, there can instantly be perceived in the mirror an effort of the organ, of which the singer himself, when he turns his attention to it, is conscious. This strain is seen and felt to increase with every higher tone, until it becomes utterly impossible to go any higher with the same action of the voice. On the other hand, when in gradually descending, keeping the action in the larynx unchanged, the lower boundary is passed, there is felt, and it is also visible, a relaxation of the organs. The tones, however, are less full and sonorous than those generated by the correct action, and it is less injurious to the voice than the transgression of the limits in the ascending scale. In correct natural singing the different registers may be recognized by certain distinct physical sensations. When the lowest tones of the chest register are sung with a moderate expenditure of breath, or are used in speaking, a tremor is felt through the whole body. This is felt coming from the place where the lungs, filled through their whole extent with air, exert a slight pressure upon the diaphragm and the parts lying below it. The sensation is less, however, as soon as the breath is exhaled with greater force, which is explained in the following manner:

FIG. V.

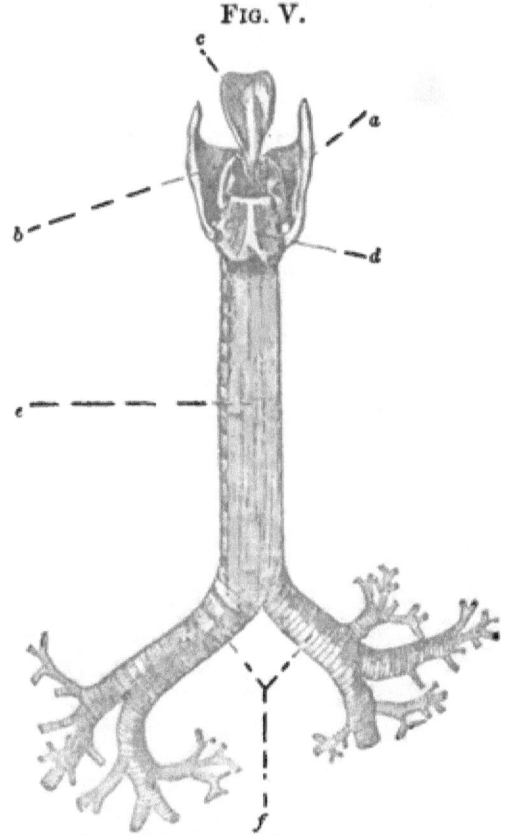

a. Thyroid Cartilage. *b*. Arytenoid Cartilage. *c*. Epiglottis. *d*. Cricoid Cartilage. *e*. Trachea. *f*. Bronchi.

The windpipe consists of cartilaginous rings connected with one another and enclosed in an elastic membrane, forming a tube terminating at the upper end in the funnel-shaped larynx. These rings in the human windpipe are not complete, but their free ends are connected posteriorly by the enveloping membrane, by means of which arrangement the windpipe may be enlarged in its transverse diameter. In producing the tones of the lowest chest register, in which the whole vocal cords are set vibrating, and the vibrations are communicated to all the interior parts of the larynx, there is needed a very copious stream of air, flowing from all parts of the lungs, so that the windpipe, *by this air alone*, is dilated as much as possible, and a sensation is created as if the whole body took part in producing the tones. In the production of the tones of the second chest register, in which the windpipe returns to its usual size in quiet breathing, the feeling is as if the tones came from the chest somewhat above the stomach. It is the place where the two bronchi coming from the lungs open into the windpipe, and where the two streams of air coming through the bronchi unite.

The tones of the first falsetto register are felt as coming from the larynx; those of the second fal-

THE VOCAL TONES. 81

setto register seem to come quite from above, in the upper front part of the mouth; and the head-tones are felt as if they came down from the forehead.

These physical sensations which, according to the difference of the registers and the various changing movements in the larynx, are so plainly felt, have given occasion to the most contradictory views in regard to the origin of the tones of the voice. But they really have no direct relation thereto. The different movements of the vocal organ require the action of different nerve-fibres and muscles by which the movements are made, and are often felt most strongly in remote parts of the body. It is, however, precisely these physical perceptions of the different registers which are an invaluable help towards the recognition of the correct use of the voice, and the avoidance of the unnatural and incorrect use of it; and for this reason I have given so particular a description of them.

In speaking, the sphere of the vocal tones is much more limited than in singing. Women use mostly the tones of the second chest and first falsetto registers, sometimes, also, those of the first chest register. Men speak an octave lower than women, and use mostly the upper half of the first chest register. In public speaking, as well as upon the stage, the second chest register is used by men, and sometimes also the lowest tones of the voice.

The most distinguished dramatic artists produce their most powerful effects with these lowest tones of the first chest register, the full, rich sound of which is best fitted to touch the tenderest chords of the soul; and in women's voices, likewise, these tones have often a wondrously touching melody.

USUAL RANGE OF THE VOCAL TONES OF WOMEN IN SPEAKING.

USUAL RANGE OF THE VOCAL TONES OF MEN IN SPEAKING.

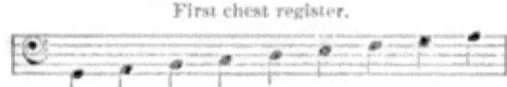

Little children speak only in the first and second falsetto registers.

In the foregoing examples the tones are designated by notes, because in speaking we have no signs **for the** vocal tones that are more exact. The tones which accompany the sounds in speech must not, however, be supposed to **be as** definite **in** regard **to** the number **of** their vibrations **as** the tones in singing. In speaking, the tones **go** up and down quite irregularly, **not at** all confined **to the** distinctly defined gradations **of** musical **tones and** intervals, but moving about in the most various ways between them.

The **most** perfect vocal tones, even in singing, **as well** as the tones **of** all musical instruments, are always more or less accompanied by noises. But, **as** Helmholtz remarks, "**in** listening **to** music **we are** not accustomed to notice the accompanying noises." The drawing of the bow across the strings of **the violin,** the striking **of** the breath against sharp edges **in** wind instruments, **etc.,** are all noises.

Without **vowel sounds it is** impossible to sing a tone, and, as has already been observed, even the most sonorous vowel sound is attended **by** noise, which, **it** is true, in a tone perfectly sung, can be heard only by great attention. **In** speaking, **on** the contrary, the noises are so prominent that we are accustomed to notice only these.

The vocal tones in speech have a very different timbre from that of the vocal tones in singing, appear duller, and have less of a clang.

CHAPTER V.

THE TIMBRE OF THE VOICE.

WE use singing or vocal tones in speaking, and we use words, or speaking sounds, in singing. Thus, in speaking, as in singing, the instrument of speech and that of vocal tones work together in a similar way; and yet there is a great difference between speaking and singing, and we immediately recognize it by the difference of the *timbre* of the vocal tones, for the timbre of the speaking sounds, as we perceive it in whispering, is as unchangeable as these sounds themselves.

It has already been stated that the pitch depends upon the number of vibrations, the fulness of the tone upon the amplitude of the vibrations, and the timbre upon their form; and, furthermore, that every musical tone consists of its fundamental tone, and of a series of overtones following one another in a certain order, and that the timbre of the tone is changed by the number and strength of these overtones; likewise, that a perfectly beautiful musical tone must be free from high *dissonant* overtones, and be composed of its fundamental tone and its *harmonic* overtones, sounding with the fundamental tone but gradually growing weaker to the last; and, finally, that to such a pure musical tone a form of vibration as round as possible corresponds. Thus, tones of the same timbre have the same number and order, and the same prominent overtones, and also the same form of vibrations.

The infinite variety of the timbre of musical instruments, as well as of human voices, is evident from the fact that the slightest change in the order, number, and strength of the harmonics, as well as the addition of dissonant overtones, has an influence upon the timbre. Helmholtz found *that the timbre depends upon the manner in which a tone begins.* When a smooth surface of water is touched, we see that it depends upon the manner in which we touch it, whether many or few little waves, or none, are formed, running out and preceding the main wave. When a little ball of lead is dropped into water, there are instantly seen running quickly out over the surface of the water, with the principal wave, and preceding it, a number of little waves (corresponding to overtones formed in the air), the rapidity of the main wave and the number of the little ones depending upon the height from which the ball is dropped. But when a bit of paper floating down through the air falls gently on the water, few or no little waves are visible preceding the main one. The same is the case when a heavy body is sunk slowly into the water.

Consequently, after long years of experience, I have learned that *for every voice in singing, the most beautiful timbre possible is to be attained only by beginning the tone with a moderate expenditure of breath, and with a quick, light, elastic touch.*

The quantity of air exhaled in the formation of a tone has likewise much to do with the timbre. It is evident from the cases we have mentioned, in which the power of speaking remained when the larynx was entirely closed, that the air contained in the mouth is sufficient for the production of speaking sounds in whispering. The vocal tones, when they are to be formed to full beautiful musical tones, require only a certain amount of breath. By a quick, light, elastic touch, a round form may be given to the waves of sound most favorable to the timbre, and for this there is needed only a weak stream of air, which may be quickly strengthened in order to broaden the waves of sound and prolong its duration. Yet while, by the broadening of the waves, the tone gains strength and fulness, the form must not be changed, as otherwise the timbre will suffer. So that the breath must be used with care if the tone, even in its greatest power and fulness, is to keep its beautiful ring.

A too strong stream of breath only disturbs the waves of sound, or prevents them from taking the form most favorable to the timbre, without giving fulness and power to the voice. For by a strong emission of the air the waves of sound are driven out only in one direction, without expanding regularly on all sides, and, instead of the low harmonic overtones which disappear, high disharmonic overtones are heard, rendering the timbre hard, sharp, and more or less disagreeable.

The difference in timbre, by which we distinguish instantly any one voice from all others, depends especially upon the fact that one, or oftener two overtones sound more plainly than the rest.

THE TIMBRE OF THE VOICE. 89

And these prominent overtones always keep the same intervals in the **series of** overtones as they **have** already been described. **If** the first and second overtones sound, *i.e.*, the first octave and **fifth, the timbre** is soft and mild, as, when the fifth and seventh sound strongly, it becomes bright and clear, etc. This is true of the voice in singing as well as in speaking, because the vocal tones are **used** in both.

The very different timbre of the same voice in singing and in speaking depends only upon the different forms **of the** sound-waves, which in singing are much more favorable **to** the timbre than it is possible for them to be in speaking, and consequently **a** greater number of **harmonic** overtones are produced. In singing, it is the vocal tones for which the cavity of the mouth is always tuned, in reference to which all the movements of the vocal mechanism, as well as all sounds of speech, must be accommodated. In speaking, on the other hand, it is the sounds of speech to which the whole resonance apparatus is fitted, and the vocal tones serve only to give to the same greater strength and reach.

For a tone in singing, the cavity of the mouth,

which serves as the resonance-tube, and which is tuned for every tone, must be more spacious than we are accustomed to make it for the same tone in speaking.

We cannot form any tone in singing without a vowel sound; but as the cavity of the mouth is tuned in singing to the vocal tone, it is scarcely possible, in many tones of the voice, to bring out certain vowels purely and plainly with a fine musical tone. It is just as impossible to sing above e upon any other vowel than *a*, and below the c upon any other than *o*, without injuring the timbre of the tone.* Every singer knows that a beautiful tone in singing often becomes possible only as the vowel sound accompanying it is pronounced a shade darker or lighter.

Thus, the breath, set into sounding vibrations in the larynx, takes in singing a direction different from that in speaking. In the formation of a tone in singing, the vibrating column of air bounds against the roof of the mouth immedi-

---

* See The Voice in Singing, page 101.

ately **above the** upper front teeth, and then rebounds, thus obtaining for its vibrations the correct form necessary to a fine musical timbre. In speaking, on the other hand, the cavity of the mouth is smaller, and the breath goes directly out before such a form of vibration can be attained; consequently, the voice in speaking has, **with many** inharmonic, **but** few harmonic **overtones, which takes from the timbre brightness** and *ring*.

But the most important difference between the timbre of the vocal tones in singing and in speaking lies **in** the time which **is** given to the vocal tones to be formed. When we sing with words, the tone rests and forms itself upon the **vowel of the** syllable, **and needs** for its development more **time** than is allowed **in** speaking, no matter how small the difference **of time may be. The** sounds of speech quickly follow **and crowd after one** another. **But for the** shortest tone in singing much more time is **required** to render it perfect. Let any one try to allow the syllables to follow one another as rapidly in singing as they do in speaking, and it **will** be seen at once that the tones instantly lose **in** melody, and their timbre becomes more like the timbre of the same tone in speaking. In like manner, the voice in speaking gains in melody when we let our words follow one another as slowly as they do in singing, and permit the voice to dwell awhile upon the vowels. When several quickly succeeding tones are to be sung, they are formed as much as possible upon one and the same syllable with one and the same vowel sound, and this is done so unconsciously that the short time which is given for the formation of such tones is not interfered with by the change in the cavity of the mouth required by the speaking sounds. In speaking, on the other hand, several syllables are generally formed upon one and the same vocal tone.

The common idea that the difference in timbre between singing and speaking arises from the fact that in speaking the tone is veiled and muffled by the noises of the speaking sounds, finds its contradiction in the fact that, in singing, the speaking sounds must be made more distinct if they are not to be veiled by the vocal tones, and if they are to be clearly understood.

The old opera-composers, with true tact, had an eye to the slurring of the words which is unavoidable in singing. Their operas consist of single pieces, arias, duets, quartettes, etc., in which, **by** simple sentences **mostly,** the sentiment of the music is supported. The speeches, dialogues, etc., **by which the** action of the piece is carried on are spoken (not sung), whereby the action is made more lively and not retarded in its dénouement. **In** place of these spoken passages, we have **now in our modern** operas the Recitative, **which is considered a great point gained, as we** thus can have **musical dramas.** But if a recitative be well sung, *i.e.*, with **the** greatest possible beauty of timbre, **the words** are unavoidably slurred and lengthened, or are uttered quickly and distinctly, and then it is impossible to produce with them a good musical tone. **A** recitative is therefore usually either badly **sung or** unnaturally spoken : hence **we may** determine the pretensions of some **modern composers,** whose operas, as **is** well known, **consist** mostly **of** recitatives, so **that a** good singer must look chiefly to the correct enunciation of the words, and treat the voice and its management as secondary matters.

The difference in timbre between the speaking and the singing voice consists, then,—

1. In the different direction of the breath.

2. In the different roominess of the cavity of the mouth.

3. In the different length of time afforded for the development of the vocal tones.

So, in speaking, the vibrations of the vocal tones have a less favorable form, and consequently also fewer harmonic overtones, than in singing.

CHAPTER VI.

REACH OF THE VOICE.

THE waves of sound, like all undulatory movements, flow out on all sides from the point at which they begin, and their amplitude decreases with the distance until it vanishes altogether. The greater or less distance which the sound-waves run through until they are lost and no longer heard constitutes the reach of the sound. It depends, like their timbre, upon how and where the tone begins, *i.e.*, upon the starting-point, and whether the air be free or confined. We see that upon a surface of water it is not the force that comes slowly in contact with it, but the quick, light, elastic touch, that sends out its undulations most quickly and farthest. Just so it is with sound. It is the sudden, elastic origin of a sound that makes it perceptible at a greater distance than when it is produced by a greater force slowly applied. For how very much elasticity increases speed and force is well known. By the elastic blow of a small hammer a nail may be driven into a board more easily than if one undertook to press it in with his whole strength; and the more elastic the motion with which a boy throws his ball, the farther and more quickly does it fly through the air.

Just so a tone will sound farther and more quickly when it can spread out unhindered from the place of its origin. Persons who form their speaking sounds far back in the mouth are not heard so far off, although they exert the greater force, as those whose words are formed in the right way: as much as possible forward in the mouth.

In relation to the Reach of Sound, modern books on Acoustics have communicated some very interesting results of scientific investigations, which may properly find a place here, as they furnish many useful hints in regard to public speaking. In a place exhausted of air no sound is possible; in rarefied air sound is weak, and when persons in a balloon have risen very high in strata of thin air, they have had difficulty in making themselves mutually understood. Prof. Saussure discharged a pistol on the top **of** Mont Blanc, and it sounded **no** louder than **a** fire-cracker. Sound **is** carried farther when it goes from below upward than when its direction is the reverse. Heat and cold, dryness and moisture of the air, have only a slight influence upon the Reach of Sound. At the freezing-point the reach of a sudden sound, as, for example, the report of a musket, is one thousand **and ninety feet** per second, and **its** speed **is** increased about **two** feet with every degree of heat. The waves of tone have the same swiftness as a cannon-ball. A beam of light that sends its waves so much more swiftly through the air would, at the above-mentioned slower rate of motion, cease to be light.

That the wind has a great effect upon the Reach of Sound is **well known;** but **not only does** the wind blowing against it lessen the reach, **but also** when **it crosses its** direction, and **when, as in a** storm, it has **the** same direction as the sound. **A** moderate wind, **on** the other hand, blowing **the** same way with the waves of sound, considerably helps the reach. Strong draughts of air in a room are very unfavorable to it. When the ventilation of the two Houses of Parliament in London was so arranged that there was a draught of air in the middle of the hall from the floor to the ceiling, it was impossible for the speakers to be heard on the opposite sides of the room.

In like manner, solid bodies which oppose the spread of the waves of sound have an obstructing influence upon its reach, and if they are of great size, they cause even a sort of sound shadow. The sound continues on the other side of such bodies, as a stream flowing towards an island reunites beyond it. We know that the smallest object standing in the way of the waves of light casts a shadow, *i.e.*, the light-waves, which are very much smaller than the waves of sound, are parted by it, and reunite at a short distance behind the object that separates them, and move on. We see also in water, that immediately beyond a large rock or island lying in the current of the waves the surface of the water is more quiet, although the large waves roll around it. So behind a large, firm body, which interrupts the sound, one hears as in its shadow far less clearly than he would if he were at that distance on the opposite side, where the waves of sound, running round it, again unite. Two persons separated by a rising ground, though they cannot see each other, may yet hear each other well; but they would hear each other better if nothing stood in the way, although the sound goes off over the elevation. Only when the sound is conducted through a pipe or a canal closed on **all sides, in which it cannot** spread itself, **is** it possible to give it any direction one chooses without the sounds **being weakened.** When solid, firmly-set bodies standing parallel in the **same** direction, such **as walls, passages, and pipes,** enclose **the sound,** the **reach of the sound is** increased, **as** the sound-waves are on one side or on all sides prevented from spreading, and they keep their form and direction longer. It is, in fact, as if the waves **found,** as it were, **a support** enabling them to run along farther and **more** quickly. **Long before the sharpest ear detects the** approach upon the highway **of a** wagon **or a troop** of horses, **the** noise may be heard **by** laying **the ear close to the** ground. **Over** the water also, music, **or** the voice in reading aloud, is **borne a** third **of the distance** farther than it is heard on land. Under the domes of churches, or in halls in which the ceilings and **the** walls make no angles, one may learn how the sound travels **along the ceiling.** When **in such places a person** in one corner whispers with his face turned to the wall, another person in the opposite corner, with his ear against the wall, may hear every word, while one in the middle of the room hears nothing. Such is the case, for example, in the great gallery under the dome of St. Peter's in Rome, in St. Paul's in London, in the great entrance-hall of the royal castle in Würzburg, and in other similar places.

The speaking-trumpets used on board of ships, the speaking-tubes in hotels, conduct the sound far beyond its usual reach, because they prevent the waves of sound from being diffused, and thus they keep their direction and form much longer when they pass through the tube, as water flowing through a pipe keeps its direction long after it has left the pipe, and before it is lost in the water into which it flows. To prove this: a speaking-trumpet of brass plate may be lined with cloth without producing any difference in the reach of the sound. That at night, not only in the populous city, but also in the lonely country, every noise is heard at a greater distance and more plainly than in the day-time, is due to the fact that by day the air is filled with all sorts of noises, which disturb the development of the waves of any single sound.

Prof. Wertheim has investigated the reach of sound through different substances. He states that water conducts sound four times more swiftly than air; lead, silver, and platinum about eight times as fast; zinc and copper, twelve; iron and steel, fifteen; glass and ice, sixteen times; and that sound is conducted by the wood of the fir-tree eighteen times more quickly than in the open air.

CHAPTER VII.

THE REFLECTION OF SOUND.

SOUND is reflected when the waves of sound strike against any object and rebound, just as it is with light; and as the beams of light are thrown back from a hard, smooth, and polished surface better and more quickly than from a surface that is rough and soft, so also firm, hard bodies best reflect sound; and, indeed, the more directly the source of the sound stands before the body reflecting it, the more acute will be the angle in which the sound is thrown back, and the more obliquely the sound-waves strike the object, the more obtuse will be the angle of reflection, the angle of incidence being the same as the angle of reflection. As it very often happens that the reflection of sound is confounded with the resonance of objects, it will be well here, for the better understanding of the matter, to state briefly what resonance is.

As a body upon which the rays of the sun fall becomes so heated thereby that **it** gives out heat **of** itself, so also many objects which are struck by **the waves of** sound become self-sounding, and mingle their proper tones with the sound received. The so-called resonance-boards, with which we are familiar in musical instruments, are all made of the wood of **the fir-tree,** as this is the only wood the fibres of which run straight without interfering with one another. These **woody** fibres begin to vibrate as soon **as** the waves of sound produced by the strings strike them, and **strengthen** thereby the thin, weak tone of the strings to the degree in which we hear it, full and strong, in our pianos and stringed instruments. On account of its resonance, fir wood is the best conductor of sound, because the sound strengthened by it keeps its own strength so much the longer. A vibrating tuning-fork sounds much stronger the instant it is placed upon wood, which immediately vibrates with it. In the human voice, as well with the noise of speaking as with the vocal tones, the resonance is the air vibrating in the cavity of the mouth, which, stirred by both noises and tones, vibrates of itself. On **the** other hand, when the sound-waves are thrown back by objects which are not themselves stirred, and do not vibrate with the sound-waves, it is Reflection. Rocks, caves, trunks of trees, grouped in certain ways, and even high billows, and sails which are rendered concave by the wind, as well as smooth walls, etc., reflect sound. Soft and elastic substances, such as carpets, heavy curtains, padded furniture, cork, rubber, and felt, dampen the sound; they do not reflect it.

To reflection is owing the well-known natural phenomenon, the Echo, which Radeau explains in the following way. We first hear the sound of our own voice, and then the reflection of the sound from some object a little later. When opposite to the reflecting object there stands another, upon which the sound that is thrown back can fall and be again thrown back, we hear the sound again somewhat later the third time, and so on. The distinctness of the echo depends upon the distance of the reflecting body from the source of the sound. According to Radeau, one cannot speak more than five to ten syllables in a second.(?) Hence if the reflecting body is so near that the sound comes back before the speaker is ready with the next

THE REFLECTION OF SOUND.

syllable, there is only a confused noise; the farther off, then, the reflecting body is, the more distinct is the echo. To hear only one syllable distinctly repeated by the echo, the reflecting body must be from ninety to one hundred and ten feet distant from the speaker, and he must utter the syllables in a manner favorable to the reach. Two syllables require twice, three syllables three times, the distance of the reflecting body. If it is farther off, there occur pauses between the repetitions. Accordingly, as the articulation of the speaker favors the reach, a distinct echo of seven syllables may be heard at a distance of four hundred or six hundred feet. When we pronounce more syllables than the echo from its distance can return to us, the first syllables are not heard at all, only the last distinctly.

We often hear in the street a noise which appears to come from quite an opposite direction to that from which it really does. When houses or walls are in front of the sound, conducting it away, we hear only the reflection from the opposite houses. All arched buildings reflect sound very strongly,* as a concave mirror reflects light.

* In the vaulted cellars of the Pantheon in Rome the

In fine, upon the same laws that are familiarly illustrated in the action of light reflected from two concave mirrors placed opposite each other, depends the reflection of sound in vaulted buildings.

The most opposite views prevail as to the way in which a room should be constructed so that the voice in singing and speaking may be best heard. The main thing in such a room must be that it shall reflect sound neither too much nor too little.

In ancient times, they had amphitheatres circular or elliptical in form, with seats all round rising step by step. These buildings had no other roofs than the sky above them, or, when it was necessary to protect them from the sun, awnings extended over them. Although they were so large, as we see in their ruins, as to hold many thousands of spectators, people seated in the highest places and most remote from the stage heard

reflection is so great that when the guide only strikes upon his clothes it sounds like the report of a gun. And in the grotto of Dionysius, in Syracuse, in Sicily, the tearing of a piece of paper resounds like the firing of a platoon of infantry.

with the greatest ease. It is evident that the ancients paid attention to the acoustic qualities of their theatres and halls. In many of their buildings of this class, it appears that there were niches, in which were hung large bells, or huge earthen vases, which, tuned to certain tones, were designed by their resonance to strengthen the sounds of the voice.

But when civilization spread over more inclement climes, and Art could no longer be enjoyed in the open air at every season of the year, a mode of building different from that of the ancients had to be resorted to.

Most of our present concert-halls, play-houses, and churches appear to be constructed not for the ear, but for the eye. The pillars, columns, galleries, boxes, pews, and prominent ornaments of all kinds, greatly interfere, as must be apparent from what has been said, with the reach and reflection of sound. Elliptical, circular, or highly-vaulted buildings are injurious to the distinct development of sound, because they have too powerful or too irregular reflection; for as two concave mirrors placed opposite each other concentrate the light upon one point, so it is with sound. That much prominent ornamentation affects the reflection of vaulted roofs and of the walls is shown in the concert-hall of the Art Academy in Berlin, and in St. Mary's Church in Dresden, which, though both vaulted, are so overloaded with decorations that the fault in their construction is in a measure remedied, and in both music sounds tolerably well.

The concert-hall of the Gewandthaus in Leipsic is celebrated for its acoustic qualities. It is about half as broad as it is long, and somewhat less in height than in breadth, and, except a gallery, it has no projecting decorations; ceiling and walls run straight, only at the farther end, where the orchestra has its place, the walls form a half-circle.

The Musical Fund Hall in Philadelphia is unquestionably the finest room in the world both for speaking and singing. It is one hundred and thirty feet long, sixty feet broad, twenty-two feet high in the corners, and twenty-eight feet in the centre, the ceiling being thus but slightly arched. Only on the long sides of the hall are there windows, otherwise the side walls are smooth. When the place is empty, and a brief, elastic tone is uttered quickly, it may be heard repeatedly from five to seven times, but very rapidly, so that the repetitions can just be distinguished. A strong tone suddenly broken off sounds long after. But when the hall is filled, and the surface of the floor is consequently covered, this reflection ceases, and every one who speaks or sings there must observe how little exertion of the voice is needed, and how beautiful and distinct is every sound.

Bearing in mind the natural laws upon which the reach and the reflection of sound depend, and what practice has taught us, it is not difficult to frame a theory according to which a room may be constructed most favorable to the distinct development of the sound. A smooth surface throws back sound just like light, in an angle; a concave surface, on the other hand, reflects all rays of light as well as all sound-waves, coming from one point, in parallel rays. It will, therefore, be seen that it is better to have only one concave surface or wall in a music-hall, as otherwise the reflection would again come to a focus, even though the sound-waves are parallel. When, therefore, there stands directly opposite to a concave. surface a flat surface from which the sound is reflected, a favorable reflection of the tone is afforded. **The size of** a building, provided **it** is not too small, has much less effect upon its acoustic properties **than** one would suppose.

In the theatres **the spectators' seats are commonly in a half-circle, because the stage with its** movable coulisses, linen and paper **walls, is** wholly unfavorable to reflection. A great fault in our modern theatres is, that sound finds so little of flat surface from which to be reflected, and the **reach of the sound is hemmed in** by numerous projecting decorations, statues, pillars, etc. **Upon almost all** stages the singers and speakers have to find and mark the places where they are to stand in order to be the most easily heard.

The Opera House in Munich has some benches in the parquette, where the reflection is **so powerful that there, instead of music, only a confused noise is heard.** A theatre renowned for its acoustic properties is an old Grecian **one** in Athens. The present Opera House **in** Venice is **also excellent** in this respect. It is built like all our modern theatres, except that instead of the open galleries for the spectators, **a smooth** flat wall decorated with paintings forms a half-circle, in

THE REFLECTION OF SOUND.   111

which are the spectators' boxes, **opened** towards the stage like windows in a house, and taking up no more space from its flat surface than windows **would.**

In the European churches there is often too much reflection, and that reflection **is** rendered irregular by the **columns,** galleries, **and decorations** upon which the sound breaks, all **of which** injures its reach **and renders the words of** the preacher often unintelligible. **In a** room with unfavorable acoustic properties, **it** sometimes suffices for the speaker or singer to change his place; but, as this depends upon the quality of **the** voice and the manner **of** speaking, **no strict rule can** be given. When it is considered **that in the** case of the loud utterance of a man's voice the sound-waves are **ten** or twelve feet **long, if it be** sought to estimate the reflection accordingly, **very often incorrect** results **will** be arrived at, **because, as we have** seen **in** relation **to** the reach and timbre **of** sound, the form as well **as** the length of the vibrations depends upon the way in which the tone begins, and this is different in different persons. Prof. Rood found that when he walked forward and backward before **a** wall **with a** tuning-fork in vibration, he came to a place where the sound could no longer be heard, and that is the point where the vibrations reflected from the wall interfere with the vibrations coming from the fork; so, likewise, a place is found where the fork sounds loudest, because the reflected waves meet with the direct waves in such a way that the latter are reinforced by the former. When a speaker finds such a place, he may be heard plainly notwithstanding the faulty construction of the room.

CHAPTER VIII.

FAULTS IN SPEAKING.

ALMOST simultaneously with the ideas which arise in the awaking mind of a child is born the power to speak the few words needed to express them. And merely by imitating the persons around him, he gradually becomes accustomed to give expression to his feelings and wishes.

As we learn speaking in childhood, so we use it all our lives, without a thought of the wonderful mechanism and perfection of the Vocal Organ. With truly inconceivable skill we unconsciously use an instrument, with which we could not possibly accomplish anything if we had, at a later period, to learn how to use it as a thing external to us. We avail ourselves of the vocal organ with just as little thought as we do of so many other miracles of creation, without troubling ourselves about their wonderful mechanism, until science directs our attention to them, and then a glimpse into the order and harmony of Nature is afforded us. Then, indeed, a feeling of devout admiration fills us, and we are impressed with a sense of a power before which, with all our wondrous intellectual faculties, we sink into insignificance.

But of what practical use is it for the speaker to understand the wonderful organism of his voice, since it has never yet occurred to any one playing upon any other instrument to trouble himself particularly about the acoustic laws of its construction, those laws in conformity with which this natural organ is also constructed? Why should we, consciously, and with painstaking, seek to change and improve what we have naturally and unconsciously become accustomed to use? The answer is this: The human voice is no common instrument, none other is so flexible and so changeable at will, and for that reason none other is so often improperly and unnaturally used.

The knowledge of the natural laws of the voice teaches us to distinguish the correct from the incorrect use of the vocal organ, the failure to distinguish which is very common, and which leads to very serious consequences, producing diseases that render speaking difficult, and sometimes wholly impossible.

And again, will not this knowledge teach us also to employ our means of speech in the best and most fitting manner, *i.e.*, to render speech more far-reaching and full-sounding, with less **effort**, and at the same time give not only the most correct but the most beautiful expression to **our** thoughts and emotions? Through **neglect of the faults and** bad habits which children, in learning to speak, catch from those around them, as also through ignorant attempts **to** improve the speaking voice, so much that is neither beautiful nor natural has gradually slipped into our manner of speaking and become habitual **with us,** that in order to be able **to** speak **well** and naturally **one must** become acquainted with the laws which **lie at the** foundation **of the** mechanism of **the** human organ **of** speech. Nature, **in** her unapproachable sovereignty, enables **us** always to produce what **is** most beautiful and most perfect, with less exertion of our physical powers than is required for **the** artificial and the unnatural.

The sounds made in speaking are, for **the reach**

of the voice, so perfectly formed when naturally produced that the arrangement therefor admits of no improvement. The characteristic noises of most of the consonants *must be formed with elastic quickness altogether forward in the mouth.* And all the rest of the consonants, as well as all the vowels, can be the most easily produced in the same way. When this takes place with the appropriate elastic abruptness, speech will have its greatest reach.

Instead of this, the noise accompanying the vowels is very frequently made slowly and feebly, more or less far back in the mouth. Even in scientific works the place for the formation of the vowels is so given that *a*, as it is pronounced in *father*, is the farthest back, and *u* (as in *lute*) the farthest front, in the mouth. The uncertain impulse which is given to the air so far back in the mouth, and by which the noise attending the vowels is made, hinders the sound from moving the external air quickly enough, and at the same time gives the voice a hollow, muffled timbre, as though the speaker had something in his mouth.

It is evident from what has just been said that

every vowel needs for its peculiar tone a certain **tuning**, which requires **a** certain definite space. **In** addition to the careless, uncertain formation **of the** vowel sound so far back, there is the common fault **of** not properly opening the mouth for the formation of the proper **tone of** the vowel, and hence is set vibrating the **air** of the nasal cavity, which**, in the correct utterance of the vowel** sounds**, is shut off by the soft palate, and the voice** thus acquires **an extremely** disagreeable nasal timbre.

As such an incorrect forming of the vowels demands a far greater expenditure of force, in the consequent effort to render the voice intelligible the speaker expels the sound with **increased** amount of breath, which naturally **is** more **fati**guing, and needlessly so. It is **evident that, in speaking,** the vocal sounds of **the glottis, even** when their sole service **is to elevate** whispering into speaking aloud, need for their development at least as much room in the cavity of the mouth as the proper tones of the vowels. The more room that is given them, the more overtones are heard accompanying the vocal tones, and the more musical and full-sounding **is** the timbre of the voice.

It cannot escape the attention of any observer that this nasal or hollow timbre of the speaking voice is very prevalent, especially in this country. But, although the **force** of life-long habit is to be contended against, it **is not so hard as one may suppose,** with due attention **and perseverance, to** overcome this fault. **The best** way **to do it is** to take pains to pronounce the vowels quickly and distinctly, in connection with such consonants as **are** formed the farthest forward in the mouth, and **then to practise with** such syllables as produce the **vowel noises** at the same place, taking care to see **that this is the case.** For **we must** remember not only **that the reach, but also, in great** part, the timbre, of **the** tones depends upon **the manner in** which the beginning is made.

I often **hear it objected, and especially by** young ladies, that **it is** ugly to open one's mouth **in speaking,** and **that the** teeth should **be** kept **closed** and the lips as quiet as possible. It is true **the** timbre **of the** sounds is injured **as** much **by** too **great an** opening of **the** mouth **as** by the closing **of the teeth. The correct** state of the **cavity of the mouth** requires only **a** moderate **opening, which, provided no needless** grimaces accompany it, **secures** graceful **and fine** speaking. With but slight movements **of** the **upper lip,** it is **the** lower jaw that, with the tongue and lower lip, **is** most moved. **The rest of the** features have nothing to do in speech, **save** as they are involuntarily affected by the import of what is spoken. It would be extremely ridiculous if **one** were to treat light **topics with a sad** countenance, **or give** expression **to pain and grief with a** smiling face.

The **characteristic noises of many of** the consonants come from expelling the breath quite forward in the mouth suddenly and with elasticity, and **at that place** where it may, unobstructed, move the external air. **Thus** produced, these noises **are favorable to the** reach, **while the** consonants *g*, *r*, *k*, and *l* can **be just as well formed** farther back **in the mouth. But it is** necessary to the **reach of the voice** that these sounds also should **have their inception** as far forward as possible. To **form** *g* **and** *k* **in** this way requires only a little attention. It is somewhat more difficult to accustom **one's** self to **a** correct utterance of *l*. It is quite common to form the spoken *l* in the way already described, with the slow movement of the edges of the tongue towards the roof of the mouth, instead of with the tip of the tongue.

With attention and practice, however, one may accustom himself to form the *l* with the tip of the tongue. But it is very difficult to form the *r* in this way if we have been used to form it with the uvula. The palatal *r*, as is so commonly heard, is formed entirely back in the mouth by the tremulous motion of the uvula. To the lingual *r*, made by the vibrating tip of the tongue, it is objected that it sounds affected; but merely because it is not usual. It can be made so lightly and softly as not to be distinguished in sound from the palatal *r*. It is evident, however, that speakers as well as singers, with whom distinctness and reach are important, should use only the lingual *r*. To learn to make it is sometimes rather difficult, but it can be done by repeating frequently and rapidly, one after the other, the syllables *hade*, *hado*, or *ade*, *ado*, *ada*, etc. In this way the tongue becomes accustomed to the right position, and the motion by-and-by becomes rapid enough for the formation of the rolling *r*. By means of the *h*, the breathing, somewhat strengthened, sets the tip of the tongue vibrating, which is raised for the **d,** if the motion is often made in quick succession. But it frequently needs years of practice to render the lingual *r* habitual.*

The thrusting forward of the tongue, which **is** so common, or lisping, as it is called, proceeds from an incorrect formation of the *s*. Instead of allowing the **tongue** to **lie near the** lower teeth, and giving free **way to the air between the teeth,** the tongue is **raised** for the *s*, as **for** the English *th*, against the upper teeth. **The** great portion of **the** narrow opening between the teeth is thus closed, so that the many dissonant overtones which **are** formed in the noise of the *s*, at the sharp **edges of** the teeth, **are so** diminished that the *s* **thus lisped** sounds like a muffled blowing, which **obtains** some degree of reach only by a comparatively greater expenditure **of breath. As** the *s*, **both** in English and in German, is very frequently **used, this** wrong method of forming **this one** sound gives to speech the very remarkable peculiarity which we call lisping. With some attention this defect may be easily corrected, especially in early youth, since it does not arise, as is commonly

* The Voice in Singing.

supposed, from any fault of the vocal organs, but is the result of a faulty habit which clings to persons the whole life long, because they never thoroughly understand the cause of it.

Another common fault, which is, however, less striking, owes its origin to the fact that too much time is given to the formation of the consonants and too little to that of the vowels. The slow, careless pronunciation of the consonants makes speech indistinct, while the slighting of the vowels, not giving time for the development of their proper tones, makes it unmelodious.

Again, we often find that indistinctness of speech is caused by the speaker's not tuning properly the cavity of his mouth for each vowel sound: this fault is invariably indicated by the insufficient motion of the lower jaw.

There exists with women as well as with men another very ugly and injurious fault, caused by contracting the soft palate and the parts lying in the back of the mouth, so that the air forcibly pressed through this narrow passage meets with unnecessary resistance. The same action takes place as in clearing the throat, only in a higher degree. This fault produces the same

FAULTS IN SPEAKING.

rattling noise, a kind of twang, which not only gives a disagreeable clang to the voice, but also tires the organs, and is often a cause of chronic sore throat.

It is not necessary to particularize the numerous bad habits of speaking which may be daily observed. Keeping in view the natural laws of speech, as we have endeavored to set them forth in the foregoing pages, every intelligent person may of himself learn to apply them. Although the incorrect formation of the speaking sounds is very tiresome, and also unfavorable to the reach of the voice, it has not by any means the injurious influence which an incorrect formation of the vocal tones has upon the vocal organs, and even upon the general health.

The different modes of formation, or rather the Registers, of the vocal tones arising in the larynx from the vibrations of the vocal cords, and accompanying the vocal sounds in speaking aloud, have been particularly described. And it has been stated that the vocal tones used in speaking in men's voices are within the limits of the low chest register.

When these tones are correctly and naturally

formed, their clang is always full, pleasing, and sonorous, and more capable than the tones of any other register of expressing the tenderest and most passionate emotions, never fatiguing the vocal organ even when the speaking or singing is long continued. But, unhappily, these fine, deep chest tones are rarely heard in singers or speakers. Instead thereof, we commonly hear them sing and speak in the so-called *Straw bass* register, which not only has a dry, raw clang, but is also extremely fatiguing, and in the same degree injurious to the vocal organs. This is mostly the cause, especially in an advanced period of life, of chronic inflammations of the throat, which defy all medical treatment so long as this unnatural mode of forming these tones is continued.

The so-called *Straw bass* register is a needless and unnatural way of enlarging the windpipe for the passage of the full column of air required for the formation of the low tones, instead of leaving this formation, as has been before described, to the air alone. The chronic inflammation, thence arising, of the vocal organs, is generally known under the name of "clergyman's sore throat." *

* See Appendix.

FAULTS IN SPEAKING. 125

That this disagreeable and injurious use of the voice **is** so common, and that even bass singers so rarely sing the deep chest tones in the natural and much easier way, is probably the reason why the false idea is so prevalent that it is only by a very powerful use of the breath and by downright bodily exertion that greater force and reach **can be** attained for the voice. Every child that amuses himself with **blowing soap-bubbles very soon** finds **out that it is only** by blowing moderately through his little pipe that the largest bubbles are **made.** And we are taught by all that has been said in the foregoing pages *that the broadest vibrations*—i.e., *the vibrations which give the strongest tones without destroying their form (timbre)— are obtained only by a quick* **and** *elastic beginning of the tone with* **but a** *moderate expenditure* **of** *breath.* When we reflect how exceedingly narrow is the opening between the vocal cords through which the breath is expelled in the formation of tones, and how delicate and slight are the vibrating cords which have to resist the air pressing upon them, it is a matter of astonishment that the vocal organ endures such **a** strain as it **is** commonly subjected to. When teachers **of** elocution and of singing require their pupils to fill **their lungs full of air, that every tone and sound may be given with the greatest possible quantity of breath and force, they require** what is just as opposite **to the purpose as it is** needlessly fatiguing, **and will be as** impossible to **be borne** as if, instead of walking, one were always to run at the top of his speed.

In all the conditions of our existence it is evident that nature has designed us to **use all our** powers in moderation. Hence when we **undertake to employ** the maximum of **our** strength in whatever **we do, as we so** often, **for** example, use our **breath** in singing and in speaking, that strength must soon be exhausted.

For the audible whispering voice **there is** always sufficient air in the mouth, **and even for** speaking aloud a moderate **increase** suffices.

Women and children, with very rare exceptions, observe the registers correctly in speaking. **The** chronic inflammations of the throat so frequent in women are mostly produced by incorrect singing of the two highest registers; and they disappear by correct singing of the second falsetto **and head registers, or by ceasing to** sing at all.

Among English-speaking people the voice is used in a very faulty manner. The reason, I suppose, is that not enough care is taken with little children to guard them against contracting bad habits of speaking. In Germany, where, in cultivated circles, special attention is given to speaking and reading, much more pains are bestowed upon the young in these particulars. The bad habits formed in childhood, so offensive to a cultivated ear, are very often overcome in after-life only with great difficulty, if they be overcome at all. In almost all our schools the teachers of elocution, to attain any valuable results, have, at the utmost, only two or three hours in a week to devote to the instruction of classes, every individual of which has faults enough to consume the time, to say nothing of the fact that too often the teachers themselves are far from speaking correctly.

A teacher of elocution should be thoroughly acquainted with the physiology of the vocal organ and with Acoustics, if he is to be successful in the hard conflict with bad habits of speech. And even then favorable results can be looked for only when a few pupils are under instruction at the same time.

An accomplished teacher will need to hear only a few words from his pupil to discover whether the vocal tones are produced in the right **registers.** By the peculiar twang **of the** voice he **will** instantly **recognize when it is unnaturally** used. **He must then first teach his pupil to form** the lowest tones correctly, in accordance with **the** physical sensations which have been described. The pupil should, with very little expenditure of **breath,** sing those tones with **a** feeling of comfort, **and without any exertion on** his part, so that the **windpipe may be** enlarged only **by** the air flowing **through it.** In singing, **the vocal** tones can be much more **easily** judged **of by the teacher, and** be much more plainly felt **by** the **pupil, than** when, obstructed by the sounds in speech, they cannot be **fully** developed. Only when these lowest tones **can be easily and** correctly sung **by the pupil should he** be required to use **them in** speaking and in reading. Every word, every **syl-**lable, every vocal sound, must be repeated until **it is** produced with perfect correctness,—not merely every vocal tone in the right register, but also every speaking sound **wholly** forward **in the** mouth, **with due** precision **and** distinctness and without a disagreeable timbre. When every sound is correctly produced, **the** pupil may advance to **reading** aloud and declamation, the teacher taking especial care that the right measure of breath **is** never exceeded.

When instruction is thus given, by **a teacher possessing** the required knowledge and **the necessary** talent, it **is surprising** how **much may be** accomplished **in a** short time; **but the** teacher **must** have **a fine** power **of observation,** great **patience and** perseverance, and a sterling general culture. **It is far** more difficult to correct a faulty way of speaking **than a faulty** way of singing, **to say** nothing of **the** expression,—giving **a soul to** the form,—of **speech. Inspired** by an indefinable emotion, one may **sing with great** effect; **but impressive** speech demands, together **with deep feeling,** a distinct **sense of the import of** what is said. A teacher of **elocution, therefore, in addition to a** thoroughly solid general **culture, must** be possessed **of the** fine feeling which will enable him to form his pupils **to** a true, natural, and beautiful delivery.

It is parents, however, who **are** bound to sow **the seeds of all that is good in the** hearts of their children, who can do the most, **and** with **far** better **results** than it is possible for a teacher **at a** later period to realize. They have but to make clear **to** themselves in what **a** correct and beautiful **mode of** speaking consists, **and to accustom** their children thereto.

Hitherto we **have** endeavored to **describe** the laws which govern the voice in speaking: **the** Form. The **giving** life and soul **to** the form of speech will **be considered in the** remaining **pages.**

CHAPTER IX.

MODULATION.

PUTTING together in close connection a number of speaking sounds, as they have now been described, we form a word whereby we give expression to some definite idea. And as we thus combine these sounds in greater or less numbers, in an infinite variety of ways, it becomes possible to us, with these few fundamental sounds of speech, to render intelligible to others every conceivable idea, every possible emotion. But even a single word, according to the vocal tones upon which it is borne, and the intonation, that is, the shade of timbre, strength, and rhythm, with which it is pronounced, may express, with the same sequence of sound, very different conditions of feeling.

There is a little comedy which has recently passed from the German to the English stage, the title of which is "Come Here." A stage-manager is represented as examining a **young actress, whom** he requires to express **with these two words every** variety of **emotion, from** the greatest joy **to the deepest sorrow and** despair. Although I had **often before seen this** little play, **it was not until I** saw Mademoiselle Janauschek **in this part that I was at all moved and made to share in the various** emotions expressed. Simply by varying the **vocal** tones, the shadowings, intonations, and *tempi* **of these** tones, the artist was able so to utter these two syllables as **to produce in the** hearer one state **of feeling** after **another of the most** different and **opposite** character, with a **success not to** be **attained** by the most elaborate and vivid description. **And** this effect was secured simply by **the** *Modulation of the Voice.*

It is commonly **thought** that melody in singing and modulation in speaking are one and the same thing. **As both** result from a series of variously arranged vocal tones, the origin and development of which depend upon the same laws, and since **to** both belong the different shades of intonation, this seems at first sight entirely correct, and hence **we see why it is** that in all works **relating** to elocution **the** attempt **is made to lay down** special rules for modulation, just as is done for melody.

Melody and Modulation, notwithstanding their apparent resemblance, are, **however, essentially** different.

Melody is the form artistically created for Song, and it alone serves **as the** Form, since Music, that airy ideal Art, has no other. The singer receives **the** melody as a thing made and fixed by **the composer,** to which he is to give life and soul; but in Speech it is the speaking sounds that constitute the Form to which soul is to be given by Modulation.

Every expression of Art requires, as well from him who represents as from him who creates it, a certain inspiration, a divine *afflatus*, **if it is to** act with any power upon others. Under such an impulse, the musical composer writes **the melody of** his work in definite characters, in notes, by which he indicates with precision the gradations of the tones, their time, and their strength. **A** melody once composed is forever unchangeable; and if a singer fails to observe with accuracy the prescribed order and time of the tones, if, indeed, he sings a single note higher or lower by only a few vibrations, a musical ear instantly detects the fault.

Melody is, therefore, a form created for Art, resting upon fixed natural laws, and in accordance with set rules. And yet, of all forms of Art it is the most delicate, incorporeal, and indefinite, by which we can give forth only obscure, indefinable moods of feeling. It is the task of the singer to animate the music as carefully as possible with the same emotions which inspired the composer who created it. The beauty of a composition is, however, not necessarily injured when the singer gives it a character natural to himself, but different from that of the composer. And here, I doubt not, we have the reason why music is so near and dear to us all. It is because Melody, the Form of this Art, adapts itself so readily to the individual feelings of every one, and gives expression to emotions as real as they are obscure.

While Melody, as the Form of Art in song, is fast bound by rules, Modulation in Speech is free and untrammelled. It is connected neither with tones depending upon a certain number of vibrations nor with intervals,* but changes with an inexhaustible variety, according to the finest

* Intervals are the greater or less distances between two notes.

shades of the emotions **from which it directly proceeds and** of which it is the immediate expression. **For the** modulation of **speech is** created at the very instant at which the **vocal sounds need it.** And as it is thus created, **it thus vanishes forever,** leaving **upon** the mind **of the hearer a more or** less distinct impression.

The **speaking sounds, arranged in syllables, words, and** sentences, constitute **the Form of Speech, animated by** modulation, **and in** characters written or printed this **form** obtains permanency, and such definiteness and exactness as no one could otherwise insure; for by means of the written or printed **word we have** exact appreciation of our thoughts, **and can even** communicate **our** feelings with comparative clearness to others, without the help **of** the voice and its modulation. For much that is addressed **to the** understanding **alone or** chiefly, **as, for example,** matters **of** science, **mere reading is often to be preferred, as it** affords **us** time **to** weigh well what **is** stated. Indeed, many dramatic works, such as Lessing's "Nathan the Wise," or Goethe's "Faust," are so **rich in** thought that they give us greater pleasure in **reading than in the** representation **on the stage,** since in the latter case many beauties, that **cannot** at once be caught, escape us. A thought, whether **heard or** read, always keeps its significance. But **the fine and deep** shades of **our** emotional **life need the** voice and the **modulation of** the vocal **tones to** give them life **and color.**

Among the millions **of** human **beings** inhabiting the globe, rarely are there to be found **two** persons so alike as not to be distinguished one from **the** other. And yet all faces are composed of **like features and** in the same manner. **The movements of the** inner nature show themselves **in the looks, and if the same** dispositions of mind often return **or** long endure, the **looks** expressive thereof become gradually **more and more firmly** set; in other words, **the** countenance **takes an** expression indicative of **a** certain **character by** which **the** individual is distinguished **and his** position **in life may be** guessed **at.** Just so **it** is with **the modulation of** the voice, which, although bounded by certain limits, is different in different individuals, and **so** distinguishes **one** from another. **As the** features **are in a** manner fashioned by the predominant states of the mind, so the Voice also comes to move, as it were, with the same intervals,

MODULATION. 137

in obedience or conformity to the life within. Like the features, the modulation of the voice is a reflection of the inner life by which persons may be distinguished and estimated. The voice of a man moved by the lower passions is certainly very different from that of a person whose voice is expressive only of true and worthy affections.

Just as there are family likenesses, and it may be known from the form and expression of the face to what nation a man belongs, so is it with the modulation of the voice. Children very readily take after their parents and kindred in this respect.

Of all nations, the Italians have the most beautiful modulation, and, altogether, they make the most correct and natural use of speech. All their speaking sounds, without exception, are made forward in the mouth; and the peculiar wealth of the Italian language in vowels, in the formation of which the mouth is always open, is the reason why the vocal tones in this language are developed far better and more musically than in any other tongue. With a natural grace Italian modulation rises and falls, like a finely-composed melody; and even when the language is not understood, it is a pleasure to listen to it from the lips of such dramatic artists as Ristori and Salvini.

The modulation of French speech, on the other hand, has a restless, eccentric character, which **is shown in the energetic way in** which, without **any reason,** single syllables are continually *accented,* and in the continuous change of the tempo. This imparts a sort of unnatural pathos, not only to the fashion of speaking on the stage, but also to the colloquial intercourse of daily life.

In Germany, **the** modulation of the **voice is** different in different places and districts. **In** Austria, **Upper** Bavaria, and Suabia it is often very pleasing. But in the **north of** Germany, especially in Saxony, it is extremely disagreeable, from the sliding of **the** voice up and down **in** the greatest intervals, oftentimes upon **one and** the same syllable.

The most monotonous is the modulation of the English. It is a favorite jest of the Italians to imitate English people in their attempts to speak Italian with closed mouth and with their monotonous modulation and accentuation.

It requires a special gift, which is granted to but few, to succeed in fully acquiring the modulation of a foreign tongue, especially in mature years. **It is by modulation that a foreigner is instantly known, even** though his speech be perfectly grammatical. While no one has ever dreamed of laying down fixed rules for the expression of **the** emotions by looks and gestures, or invented, for the understanding of such rules, written characters, all works on Elocution undertake, **what is just as** impossible, **to** give numerous **rules for** the modulation of the voice, often enough **contradictory, and to teach in** what intervals **the** voice is **to be** modulated for this or that effect. We frequently meet with propositions and attempts to devise for this purpose some peculiar system of notation. **Many** writers have indeed endeavored to indicate **the** modulation of single sentences by notes, as in music. Of the success **of** such attempts the following specimens may enable the reader to judge. We premise only that modulation in speaking does not, like melody **in** singing, keep to distinct limited tones, but ranges by manifold gradations between the tones, which obviously cannot be indicated by notes. **Of** a number of persons who have attempted, at my request, to read aloud such sentences according to the notes here given, not any two modulated them in the same way; and it was only after long-continued and laborious practice that the above notation could be observed.

From "*Die Grundrisse der körperlichen Beredsamkeit.*"

Wenn ich mit Menschen und mit Engelzungen redete und hät-

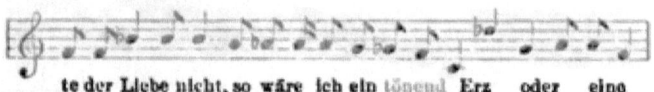
te der Liebe nicht, so wäre ich ein tönend Erz oder eine

klingende Schelle. Sie ist da. Sie ist da. Ist sie da?

Sie ist da. Er ist mir gut. Ist er mir gut? Er ist mir gut.

Hänle.

Kannst du sie lieben? O du mein Alles. O Freund, wer kann es ändern?

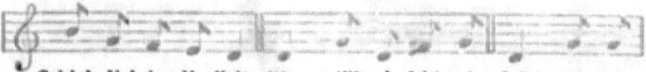
Schick dich in die Zeit. Wer will's befehlen? Ich will nicht!

Ist es dir Ernst? Recht gerne, Recht gerne, Recht gerne.

MODULATION. 141

Rush.

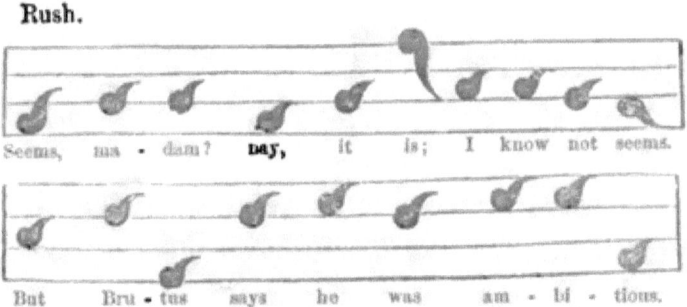

Dr. Rush is of the opinion that for a proper modulation in speaking it is necessary to raise or lower the voice within greater or smaller intervals on each syllable. This he has endeavored to express by peculiar notations, as will be seen in the above example. The thicker part of these notations he calls *radicle*, and denotes by it the principal and accentuated part of the interval; while the thinner he calls *vanish*, in order to express the gradual dying out of the intensity of voice. Many rules are given in his work as to how this sliding up and down of the voice shall be accomplished according to the different emotions which are to be expressed. Dr. Rush has apparently noticed the proper tones of the speaking sounds, but, like all those who have occupied themselves with this subject, has treated the speaking sounds in connection with, instead of distinguished from, the vocal tones, and both as resulting **from** one action **of** the vocal organs.

On account of the great variety of the proper tones of speaking **sounds, and** their **rapid** changes, **it is very necessary, for a beautiful manner of** speech, **that the vocal tones should move in slow intervals, and never, or very rarely, change their pitch on the** *same syllable.*

What notes are to Music, written or **printed letters are to** Speech; **and it is by means of notes that Music and by** means of letters **that Speech are both made** permanent, and **more than this we do not need. To** the animation **of the Form of** Speech, **which Form** we have **in the** speaking sounds, **in a word, to** Modulation, we **look not only for the** due combination **and pitch of the vocal tones, but also for the** stronger **or weaker** accentuation, as well as for the time, **or** the slower or quicker manner **in** which **the** syllables, words, **or** sentences are **uttered.** The accentuation of his **speech, as well as the** import of what he says, intimates to the speaker that he must dwell upon the **long, low syllables longer or** pronounce them more strongly than the light, short syllables, and thus he will **utter more slowly and** accentuate more emphatically those words which especially indicate his meaning. When the object is merely **to** address the understanding **and** communicate thought, accentuation is the main thing. All subordinate propositions **are** stated quickly and lightly, **in** order to dwell emphatically upon the principal thought and thus to impress it **upon the** mind of the hearer. Less depends in **this case** upon the order **of the vocal** tones, or **upon the** melody **of** speech. **But when** emotion **is to be** expressed, **it** is, together with the accent and the **time,** the melodious order of the vocal tones, particularly the manner in which they rise and fall, which is chiefly **to** be regarded. As **in** singing, and in every kind of music, **feelings** and moods can **be** expressed more deeply and delicately than **by any** other **art,** so **also** the Modulation **of** the Voice, the musical tones **of** speech, although they cannot be as perfectly developed as in Song, are yet capable in like manner of giving expression to every emotion, and of awakening it in the hearer, provided always that the speaker himself is entirely possessed with it. "The dramatic artist," says Lessing, "must show, by the surest and most correct tones, that **he is** thoroughly penetrated with the meaning of his words. Even a parrot must be taught right accentuation. How wide the difference between an actor who merely understands a passage and one who feels as well as understands! Words, the meaning of which has been committed to memory, may be very correctly spoken even when the mind is occupied with quite other things, but in this case no feeling is possible. The soul must be wholly present, its attention must be directed singly to the expression of the words. The differences in the modulation of voices are infinite, and, although they cannot be classified or defined, they can be distinguished by the most unpractised ear, as well as observed by the most uncultivated voice, when the voice comes from a full heart."

"In declamation," says Goethe, "I must put off my own native character, deny my own nature, and transport myself into the situation and mood of him whose rôle I act, so that I shall feel every emotion as he felt it."

The public speaker and the dramatic artist must thus, above all things, be profoundly impressed and penetrated with the sentiments which they express before they can hope to produce any

MODULATION. 145

effect upon their hearers. The mind is so accustomed to rule the body, and to make the bodily movements subservient to its affections, that every one, according to the measure of his sensibilities, may command a more or less effective modulation of his own voice. **The more deeply** we ourselves feel **what** we seek **to say, the** more surely **shall we** communicate the same feeling to others, **and the more** correctly and **unconsciously shall we avail** ourselves **of the** inexhaustible means of expressing ourselves, afforded **by** the modulation of the voice. We frequently meet, however, with very amiable and highly-cultivated persons with a very bad and affected modulation of the voice, contracted usually from those around them, in early life, and which has become so fixed that **they have** lost all sense **of its** disagreeable character, and consequently **have** retained the evil habit through life. **It is indeed** very difficult to get rid of a bad habit, **but it** is not impossible. By attention and perseverance grimaces and awkward gestures may **be** corrected. Easily and successfully, however, **as** one's manner of speaking may **be** improved and bad habits corrected (that is, so far as the speaking sounds, which are subject **to** certain fixed laws, are concerned), the modulation of the voice is another affair, since *it is not to be governed by rules.* Only indirectly, by example, by general culture, and by all those means of education which tend to elevate and refine our sensibilities, can the modulation of the voice be wrought upon and improved. The most can in this case be done by parents, who should tolerate in their children no disagreeable ways of modulation.

But what constitutes a beautiful Modulation of the Voice?

It must be evident to our readers that we have already virtually answered this question. Our aim in the preceding chapters of this book has been to analyze and describe the speaking sounds, and to show wherein their correct articulation consists. There our office, as regards elocution, ends. Modulation comes from a higher and deeper source than the organ of the voice. Let the mind be fully occupied with the thought, or the heart full to overflowing with the emotion that seeks utterance, and the voice may be trusted to take care of itself. To lay down rules for modulation is as idle as to undertake to subject to regulation the features of the face, to teach that the brows must be knit when anger is to be expressed, or the corners of the mouth drawn down in the expression of grief. The only rule in regard to such things, the modulation of the voice with the rest, is stated in the familiar words of the Roman poet,—"If you wish me to weep, you must weep yourself."*

The calling, and the success, of the great artists of the drama lies in this, that by the inspiration of their genius they transport themselves into the situations and hearts of the characters which they represent. When this is done, the play of the features, all the movements of the body, and all the tones of the voice, will follow as they should. Let the speaker cultivate the sense of the beautiful and the graceful, as it was cultivated of old by that wonderful people whose temples and statues and literature have been the wonder and the models for centuries down to this hour, and, inspired by that, and by the faith or emotion swelling for utterance, he need not trouble himself about modulation.

But where the right feeling, the true impulse, is wanting, affectation, extravagance, and servile

* "Si vis me flere, dolendum est primum ipsi tibi."—Hor.

imitation **are sure to** creep in and deprave **the** finest powers **of** speech. And so it comes **to pass** that the extraordinary and the odd usurp the place **of** the beautiful; and **this is** the case not only in matters **of fashion, but also in art.** Everywhere one **is** painfully impressed with **this lack of** good taste only too frequently apparent in **public speakers** and dramatic representations. Play-actors **are** almost always most vehemently applauded when **their** delivery is most unnatural and extravagant. **How often does** one hear even popular actors using **on** the most trivial occasions the same deep tones **that** belong, on **the stage, to the** production of **the** most tragic effects! **At** the beginning **of the** present century such unnatural declamation was all but universal on the German stage, and **was** considered as a grace even in ordinary **conversation.** Within **the last** twenty years **the** critic (thanks to him!) has fallen mercilessly upon this affectation and exaggeration of the German theatres, **and** in so doing has exercised a good influence **upon** the popular taste: so that **now** the most distinguished dramatic artists **of** the present day study **to be** natural, recognizing truth and nature **as the soul of Art.**

Among many preachers also there prevails a highly unnatural and offensive modulation of the **voice,** the so-called pulpit tone, a sort **of** monotonous sing-song, in which, in almost every sentence, the voice rises and falls in the same way, closing with a downward movement.

The pulpit tone appears **to be traditional, and to** have come down from the Past, as **the consecrated** mode of expressing the sacred **and the** solemn.

And yet **it is** the preacher especially, whose calling it is to exercise a forming influence upon his hearers, who should be so thoroughly pene**trated** with the truth and importance of what he has **to say,** that his voice will **be naturally** and involuntarily modulated aright. **Many** preachers have a habit of speaking very rapidly, **which is as little** fitting **in a** church **as the** frequent unnecessary changing of the register, the making of long pauses in order to arrest attention, when nothing of any weight follows; and other tricks for effect. How deeply, on the other hand, is one impressed, and how elevating is the effect, when the preacher, having spared no pains in the acquisition of distinctness and melody in pronunciation, gives utterance naturally, spontaneously, with a true modulation of the voice, to that which he himself feels deeply!

As oftentimes one melody is sung more easily than another in the same pitch, because the composer knew how to choose the vowel sounds which are most favorable to the notes, so there are writers whose works are more easily read than those of others, and seem of themselves to suggest and inspire a beautiful modulation. Upon a critical examination it will be found that these readable writers have the tact to cause dark and bright syllables so to alternate that even their prose has a certain rhythm, *i.e.*, a pleasing sequence of long and short syllables. Those poets whose education has made them intimate with the Greek language are for the most part distinguished for their flowing style: Schiller, for example, in whose poems the German language is used in a way most favorable to modulation. Likewise in Evers's romance "Die ägyptische Königstochter" we have a style which for its beautifully flowing character can hardly find its equal in German literature. On the other hand, writers who look only to the grammatical relations of their words often fail to command due interest from their readers by permitting syllables of like sound to follow one another, and by not properly distributing long and short syllables, faults easily to be avoided by every one who has discernment enough to see them. Everybody is familiar with series of syllables of like sound, which it requires considerable practice to pronounce with any degree of rapidity.* By an alternate action of the organs of speech changing readily and without interruption, and by a correct use of long and short, dark and bright, syllables, a kind of modulation is formed of itself. A public speaker may thus by careful preparation do much to secure a pleasing delivery.

Parents and teachers should especially look with care to the formation in the young not only of a correct but also of a beautiful manner of speaking. And it would surely do no harm if, after the example of the Greeks, more pains were taken in the education of children, to awaken and cultivate in them the sense of the beautiful, which not only renders life so much richer and more

* Peter Piper picked a peck of pickled peppers, etc.; or, Theodore Thistle sifted a sieve of unsifted thistles, etc.

graceful, and lifts us above so many petty cares, but also gives to the soul a higher and nobler aim. If this book helps in any degree to effect this object alone, the pains bestowed upon it will be sufficiently rewarded.

APPENDIX.

APPENDIX.

CLERGYMAN'S SORE THROAT.

In the foregoing pages the way has been shown in which our organs act in order to produce speech; and it has also been shown that scientific principles underlie and govern all those various sounds and noises which are necessary to speech. But, as in a great many other things, so also in speaking and singing, natural laws have been disregarded or even denied altogether, and by false training an artificial and unnatural way of speaking has been formed by many of our orators and singers. Nature, however, revenges herself severely for any disregard of her laws, and the result of this artificial mode of speaking is, that the vocal organs very often become diseased. In the following pages the attempt will be made to state precisely the nature of the disease thus occasioned, and the mode of treating it.

Many names have been given to this particular form of throat disease, as, *follicular pharyngitis, papillary sore throat, clergyman's sore throat*, or *contenda phonia*, as Dr. Gibb calls it.*

It is most common among those whose calling it is to speak or sing in public, or who are obliged to speak for a considerable length of time daily, such as auctioneers, school-teachers, etc.

The first symptoms perceived are a dryness of the mucous membrane of the pharynx and a peculiar huskiness of the voice. These symptoms become gradually worse; a hacking cough sets in, which, through its persistence, is very annoying; the voice becomes more and more husky, and frequently is lost altogether, and attempted phonation becomes painful. There is little or no expectoration.

A careful examination, with the aid of the laryngoscope (which is indispensable, and without which no correct diagnosis can be made), reveals the following condition of the parts: the soft palate appears relaxed and of a darker hue than in health, with the uvula slightly elongated and

---

* Gibb, Diseases of the Throat and Windpipe. London, 1864.

swollen. **The** mucous lining of the pharynx is **dry and** injected, and in cases of long standing studded with enlarged follicles, and sometimes small ulcers are seen on its surface. Upon introducing the mirror into the mouth and lifting with it the uvula, the interior of the larynx is brought into view. The epiglottis, the first object seen, **is** swollen and injected, with here and **there an enlarged** follicle on its posterior surface. The arytenoid cartilages are swollen and inflamed, with an abrasion **or even** ulceration between them. The vocal cords are reddened and thickened, especially **at** their free border. **A** slight paralysis of the cords, and especially of the left cord, is present, which **is** shown in the laryngoscopic image by an inability of the cords **to meet** in the median **line.** When **it is** possible **to** gain insight into **the** trachea, its lining mucous membrane is found to **be** congested and thickened, **as** is the case with that of the larynx and pharynx.

These are the conditions of the parts in typical cases of this disease; but, of course, all the symptoms may be aggravated in severe cases, where, sometimes, the ulcerations extend into the trachea **and** up into **the** nasal cavities, involving the Eustachean tubes and the middle ear in a general sub-acute inflammation.

The patient, like most writers on this subject, gives as the cause of the disorder some exposure to a cold draught of air while using his voice or immediately after. Sometimes, however, he is not able to refer the beginning of the trouble to any particular time or exposure, but describes it as having come on gradually. The latter is, as will be seen, the correct statement as to the origin of the disease, for, the predisposition existing, the slightest cause suffices to develop the symptoms.

The real cause, which lies at the foundation of the disease, and which the physician has to remove in order to effect a permanent cure, consists not, as many suppose, in a long-continued use of the vocal organs, but in a faulty way of using them. The voice, rightly managed, may be used in speaking or singing all day long without any other consequence than a feeling of bodily fatigue.

In this volume, as well as in "The Voice in Singing," the divisions of the human voice into registers, and their mechanism and extent, have been fully explained, and it is therefore not necessary to dwell here upon these facts. Taking it for granted that they are fully and clearly understood, I proceed at once to the consideration of the cause of the so-called "clergyman's sore throat."

Men speaking correctly use the first and rarely the second series of the chest register, women and children mostly the second chest and the first falsetto register.

The action of the first series of the chest register, it will be recollected, consists in setting the vocal cords into full and loose vibrations, and in dilating the trachea by means of the pressure of the air from the lungs while the arytenoid cartilages move to and fro.

The trachea can, however, be dilated in its transverse axis by compressing it in its longitudinal axis, which is effected by the large muscles of the neck, as will be understood by referring to the drawing of a dissected neck.

This dilating of the trachea by muscular effort is what is done by most public speakers. The result of it is, that the larynx is drawn forcibly down and compressed, and so its relation to the cavity of the mouth is altered and the free ac-

APPENDIX.

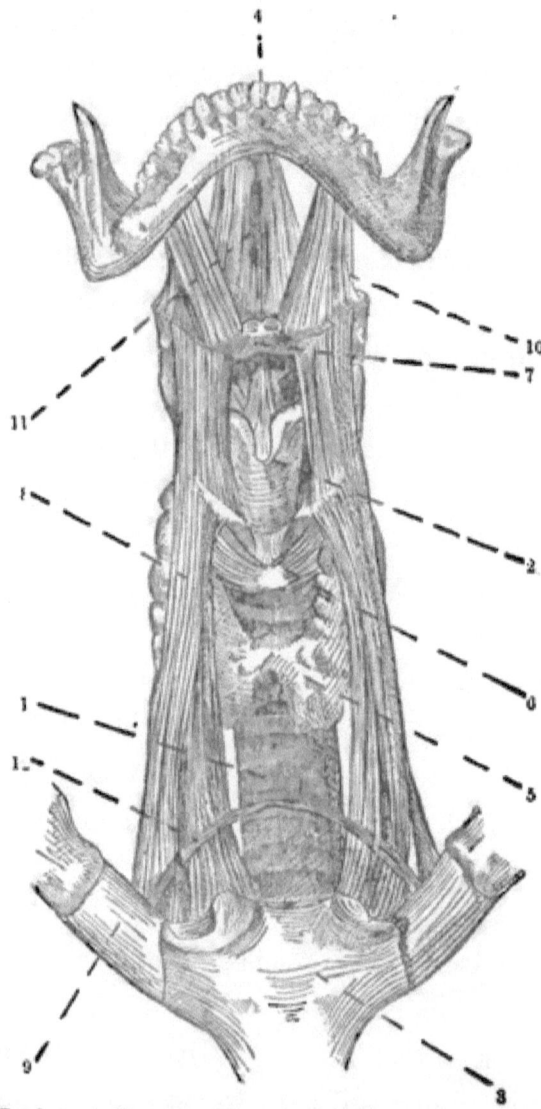

1. Trachea. 2. Thyroid Cartilage. 3. Sternum. 4. Lower Jaw. 5. Thyroid Gland. 6. Crico-Thyroid Muscle. 7. Hyoid Bone. 8. Sterno-Thyroid Muscle. 9. First Rib. 10. Hyoglossus Muscle. 11. Genioglossus. 12. Transversus Colli Muscle (exceptional). (*Luschka*, "*Anatomy of Larynx.*")

tion of the small muscles of the larynx prevented. Consequently there is a straining of the tensor muscles of the larynx to keep the vocal cords stretched tightly enough for the required pitch. In order to assist those muscles in their hard task, an additional pressure is put by the expiratory muscles upon the air contained in the lungs, which presses upon the vocal cords, and, besides setting them into vibration, renders them at the same time more tense. This can easily be observed in the mirror, and the effect of the undue pressure upon the delicate white bands shows itself in the shape of a faint red line along the edges, which gradually extends over their whole surface if the strain is kept up, indicating a congestion of the parts. It disappears again, however, when they are rested. The undue amount of breath used, in escaping through the glottis with considerable force, produces a friction sound, or slight rattling, by setting the various folds of mucous membrane in the mouth and the uvula into irregular vibrations.

The Germans use the expression "*Straw bass*" to designate this peculiar way of speaking or singing. The noise accompanying the voice bears a striking resemblance to that made by loose straw falling upon a hard surface.

It is not surprising, therefore, that when the strain is kept up frequently for a considerable time the congestion does not disappear, but, on the contrary, is increased to a sub-acute inflammation, which gradually extends over the whole surface of the mucous membrane lining the larynx and pharynx, and that a change in the nutrition of the parts takes place.

In the treatment of this disease two steps are to be taken: first, the medicinal and topical; and second, the gymnastics of the voice.

The medicinal part of the treatment consists in touching the ulcers and enlarged follicles with a solution of nitrate of silver, from twenty to eighty grains to an ounce of water, or with some astringent solution, according to the state of the inflammation. Ulcers in the trachea are very difficult to reach, and therefore powdered alum or tannic acid with gum arabic may be blown into the trachea, the amount of the powder, however, not exceeding ten grains. The touching is most easily effected with a fine camel's-hair brush mounted on a silver wire or probe, which must be bent at the angle required to reach the spot. In these operations the laryngoscope is indispensable, as only the ulcers and follicles should be touched. A general swabbing of the throat, so commonly practised, should be abstained from, as an operation not only disagreeable and painful but also doing more harm than good. In order to relieve the dryness of the pharynx, inhalations of tar-water, tincture of benzoin, balsam of Tolu, and remedies of this class may be administered by means of the steam atomizer, or, better still, by an inhaling-bottle, as these substances tend to clog the fine opening of the atomizer tube.

The paralysis, if such exists in the cords, generally disappears with the other symptoms; if not, the application, internally, of an induced current of electricity of moderate strength will remove this difficulty also.

As soon as the parts begin to assume a healthier appearance, the gymnastics of the voice should be begun, and the patient should be practised in using his voice according to the natural laws laid down in this work and in "The Voice in Singing," selecting for practice such words and syllables as are most suitable to the case.

APPENDIX.

No strict rules can be given, as, in every case, the injury to the voice is accompanied by some peculiar fault in speaking. The course which I have found most efficient is to teach the patient, with the aid of a piano, and for a few minutes only at a time, to sing and speak in the natural divisions of the voice, using as little breath as possible. As soon as he has attained any certainty in the proper use of the registers, he is required to read aloud or recite some verses; every word which he does not pronounce properly being corrected, those consonants and vowels are selected for practice at home in the pronunciation of which he is most deficient. This must, however, not be continued too long at a time: from five to ten minutes will be sufficient at first.

The length of time required until the patient is able to speak correctly, without falling back into his old habits, depends greatly upon his fidelity and application in acquiring this, to him, new mode of speaking. Time only is needed to effect a permanent cure.

C. SEILER, M.D.

www.ingramcontent.com/pod-product-compliance
Lightning Source LLC
Chambersburg PA
CBHW030254170426
43202CB00009B/732